Good News from Matthew

Volume 2

Volume 2

GOOD NEWS FROM MATTHEW

Malcolm O. Tolbert

Broadman Press
Nashville, Tennessee

4213-53 (paperback)
ISBN: 0-8054-1353-7

4281-26 (BRP, Volume 1)
4281-27 (BRP, Volume 2)

Library of Congress Catalog Card Number: 75-2537
Dewey Decimal Classification: 226.2
Printed in the United States of America

Volume 2

CONTENTS

CONTENTS

Foreword

We asked Dr. Tolbert to do an exposition of Matthew that would bring out its meaning and message for today. We wanted a book for Bible students rather than scholars. This commentary, therefore, does not deal extensively with technical and critical problems. It will be especially useful to the Sunday School teacher and preacher who are attempting to interpret the Gospel for people as they live in today's world.

Although this is not a verse-by-verse treatment of the Gospel, it does not ignore any verses. The two volumes of *Good News from Matthew* are divided into twenty-three chapters. Each chapter has several sections, each one dealing with a group of verses, consecutively through the Gospel. A brief, indented paragraph opens each section to summarize its content. Then the interpretation of the passage is presented under two or more subheads. Thus, the teachings of Matthew are readily available to the reader with an open Bible.

Dr. Tolbert is a capable New Testament scholar. He has an earned doctorate, was a teaching missionary in Brazil for nine years, and has been teaching New Testament and Greek at New Orleans Baptist Seminary since 1961. This is his fourth book, plus his interpretation of "Luke" in *The Broadman Bible Commentary*. He is thoroughly acquainted with the literature on Matthew.

THE EDITORS

12.
You Are the Son of God

14:1 to 16:4

I. The Death of John the Baptist (Matt. 14:1-12)

When Herod hears about Jesus, he concludes that he is John the Baptist raised from the dead. The circumstances of John's death are narrated.

1. The circumstances of John's death. Herod Antipas, the son of Herod the Great, was made ruler over Galilee and Perea after the death of his father in 4 B.C. John's denunciation of his adulterous relationship with Herodias came at a particularly difficult time for the Galilean ruler. Herod Antipas was in trouble with Aretas the king of the neighboring Arabians (Nabateans). His first wife had been Aretas' daughter, and he had deserted her when he became enamoured with Herodias on a trip to Rome. This naturally angered Aretas.

Herodias was a niece of Herod Antipas and also the wife of his brother. This brother is identified as Philip in the text. Josephus, however, tells us that Philip's wife was Salome, the daughter of Herodias. Some ancient manuscripts omit Philip from verse 3 and read "his brother's wife." From other sources we learn that Herodias' first husband was called Herod Boethus. Whether he was also called Philip we do not know.

Herodias was also incensed by John's criticism of her unlawful and immoral relation with her brother-in-law (see Lev. 20:21). The Greek text of 14:4 allows the translation: "John kept on saying to him." John just would not be quiet about the matter. Herodias wanted to silence John permanently. When Salome, the daughter of Herodias, pleased Antipas with her dance, the opportunity to get rid of the prophet presented itself. She prompted Salome to ask for the head of John the Baptist. Herod felt constrained to grant the request since he had vowed to give her anything she asked.

2. *Herod's reaction to Jesus.*   Men's voices may be stilled by violence, but a guilty conscience is not so easily silenced. The news about Jesus' ministry raised the spectre of John the Baptist for the troubled Herod. Was this John the Baptist returned from the dead to disturb him again?

It may be that Herod believed John had actually been raised from the dead. Or, he may have concluded that the spirit of John was reincarnated in Jesus. There was much similarity, as we know, between the message of Jesus and John. Both were heralds of the kingdom, and both called the people to repentance.

One of the lessons of this episode, as well as of many others in the Bible, is that the work of God goes on. A prophet is raised up by God to proclaim his message. People react violently and destroy him. But another stands in his place! The truth of God marches on. His plans are not defeated by violent men.

Some of the many questions we have about John have to do with the way his ministry touched Jesus' own life in important but not fully explained ways. The news of John's death apparently caused Jesus to withdraw from Galilee (14:13). Perhaps he perceived that Herod might kill again to still the voice of the one whom he believed to be a resurrected John.

II. Miraculous Episodes (Matt. 14:13-36)

Jesus withdraws to an unpopulated area, followed by the crowds. He feeds them miraculously by multiplying five loaves and two fish. He sends his disciples across the lake by boat. When a storm arises in the night, he comes to them, walking on water. When Peter attempts to walk to Jesus on the water, he begins to sink and is rescued by Jesus.

After they land, Jesus heals many who are brought to him on the plain of Gennesaret.

1. The feeding of the five thousand. This miracle is the only one found in all four Gospels, which may indicate something about its importance to the early church. The narrative is straightforward and clear. Jesus went into a "lonely place," an uninhabited region, perhaps to get away from Herod Antipas. The crowds followed him, and he healed their sick. At the end of the day the disciples suggested that the people be dismissed to find food in nearby villages. But Jesus rejected their suggestion. He took five loaves and two fish and fed the crowd, which numbered five thousand men in addition to women and children. Enough was left over to fill twelve baskets, perhaps one basket for each of the twelve.

Many scholars tie this miracle to the practice of the Lord's Supper. They point out the similarities between Jesus' actions here and those at the institution of the Last Supper. Normally, however, a Jewish meal was begun in the fashion described here. The head of the family began the meal with the blessing over the bread, a brief prayer of thanksgiving. He then distributed pieces to others around the table. The relation to the Lord's Supper, therefore, is not established.

Still others see in the meal a connection with the messianic banquet of the end-time. Jesus made it a practice to eat with his disciples, and the early church continued the practice of the fellowship meals. They had a significance for the future, for they symbolized the fellowship of the redeemed at Messiah's table. If the miracle is a symbol of the heavenly banquet, however, it is not made clear by the text.

We may be on firmer ground when we understand the miracle as a revelation of the person of Jesus. God through Moses had fed Israelites in the desert. One aspect of Jewish messianic expectation was that the Messiah would care for his people in similar fashion.

2. Jesus walks on water. The narrative tells us that Jesus made the disciples get into a boat and leave, while he dismissed the crowd. John gives us some insight into the situation when he tells us that the crowds on this occasion wanted to make Jesus a king by force (John 6:15).

The crowds had perceived the meaning of the miracle. Jesus was the King Messiah. They wanted to force him to take his rightful place as David's heir But Jesus would have none of it. He was the Messiah, but not the kind the people imagined. He dealt with the problem by making the disciples leave. Were they stirring up the people to make him king? Then Jesus went into the hills to pray after he had dismissed the crowds.

Perhaps Jesus felt the need for prayer after the events of such a turbulent day. Perhaps he needed to be alone with God to reassess his own commitment and redefine his own methods and goals.

While the disciples were rowing across the Sea of Galilee, which was about four and a half miles wide at that point, they were overtaken by a storm. Unable to make progress against the wind, they were frustrated and helpless. But Jesus came to them in the fourth watch, that is, between 3:00 and 6:00 A.M. The Romans divided the night into four watches.

Jesus greeted his frightened and defeated followers with the phrase: "It is I." Literally translated, he said: "I am." This is the phrase that is used as a self-revelation of God (Ex. 3:14). In John's Gospel Jesus uses it often of himself (e.g., John 4:26; 18:6). Perhaps something of this meaning is involved here. The disciples experienced the abiding presence of the Lord in the night in the midst of the storm.

Once again we must ask what this story meant to early Christians and what it means to us. They did not expect Jesus to come walking to them on water during a literal storm. Neither do we. But believers have often felt helpless and frustrated when caught in the circumstances of life. And over and over again they have experienced the presence of their Lord, calming the storms and bringing them safely to shore.

3. Peter's attempt to walk on water.   The narrative is probably a biographical cameo of Peter. His impulsive attempt to go to Jesus is certainly characteristic of what we know of Peter. Also his inability to do what he thought he could do reminds us of his failure in the last hours of Jesus' life (see Matt. 26:33).

He was only a "half-believer," a man of little faith. He had enough to get started but not enough to carry him through. But in his failure he experienced the saving power of Jesus, which after all is the only sure hope of any disciple. Jesus helped him to get back in the boat.

4. The confession.   "You are the Son of God" was the response of the worshiping disciples to the Lord who had come to them in the night and stilled the storm. This is the highest confession they could make.

III. Controversies with the Religious Leaders (Matt. 15: 1-20)

The Pharisees and scribes criticize the disciples for not washing their hands before eating. Jesus accuses them of circumventing the will of God through their oral traditions. Jesus teaches that true spiritual defilement comes from within the person rather than from the outside.

1. The cause of the controversy.   The tradition of the Jewish elders was transmitted orally during the time of Jesus. This oral tradition had as much authority for the Pharisees as did the written law. They taught that it also was originally imparted by God to Moses.

The written law of the Old Testament did not command people to wash their hands before eating. This was part of the oral law. Washing the hands was supposed to remove defilement which might be incurred by touching something or someone ritually unclean. The Pharisees believed that they would be defiled or rendered unclean if they ate with unwashed hands that had come into contact, for example, with a Gentile.

The Pharisees, along with the scribes who were the recognized experts in the law, probably constituted a delegation sent from Jerusalem. Perhaps they were under orders to investigate Jesus, his teachings, and his practices.

Jesus was a Jew. In the main he was faithful to Jewish law and institutions. But he had a prophetic approach to religion which prevented a slavish obedience to contemporary interpretations and practice. Passages such as this one show us that Jesus did not place a high value on the oral traditions. This was due to his prophetic insight which we can also perceive in this passage. If the disciples did not wash their hands before eating, it must have been because Jesus perceived the basic error on which the practice was based. A man's personality may defile him, but his failure to observe ceremonies will not make him bad.

2. Jesus' reaction to the criticism.   Jesus made two points about the oral laws. In the first place, he pointed out that in certain instances they were used to circumvent the true will of God.

He gave one example. In the Ten Commandments God commands men to honor their parents. One way of honoring them was to care for their physical needs in illness or old age. Men, however, could avoid their obligation to a parent by vowing to dedicate what they had to God. Evidently they could continue to use their own property for themselves in the meantime. Jesus interpreted this kind of oral tradition as a fulfillment of Isaiah's prophecy (15:8, cf. Isa. 29:13). Instead of being God's laws, as taught by the Pharisees, they were really precepts of men.

Jesus said that this "dedication" was a violation of God's law. It should be said that by the end of the first centuries the rabbis taught that the commandment to honor one's parents took precedence over any such vow.

In the second place, Jesus taught that many of the traditions involved a basic misunderstanding of genuine morality. Men were not defiled by what they put into their stomachs. Eating food without washing their hands, therefore, did not make them unclean before God.

This religious principle, of course, has a broad application. Most Christians have understood it to be relevant to the food laws written into the Old Testament. Man is not defiled by eating pork or any of the forbidden foods of the Old Testament.

The Christian approach to food and drink is not based upon ritual. It is based instead on fact. If a food is detrimental to one's health, it is an exercise of mature judgment to avoid it. Furthermore, if what we take into our bodies causes us to act in irresponsible or immoral ways, it should be avoided.

Genuine morality has to do with what a person is on the inside. It has to do with character. What comes out of a man is an expression of what he really is. Immoral acts are an indication of inner moral corruption or defilement. The list of sins mentioned by Jesus in verse 19 is drawn from the Ten Commandments: murder, adultery, fornication, false witness, and slander.

3. *Two approaches to religion.* What we see in the passage is a fundamental clash between two opposing attitudes toward religion. The one emphasizes the outward and is concerned mainly with ceremonies; the other emphasizes the inward and is concerned mainly with the quality of a man's life.

We must recognize that this battle is never completely won. Even Christians face the persistent, perennial temptation of betraying their Lord by putting the major emphasis on ritual. I often hear my students say about a member of their church: "Brother John is a good man." And then they add: "He comes to church and he tithes." But a man may come to church and tithe and still be arrogant, selfish, a gossiper, or immoral sexually, as we all know through tragic experience.

4. *The reaction to Jesus' teaching.* According to the disciples, "the Pharisees were offended" by Jesus' position (15:12). Their anger was caused by their recognition of the inherent threat to their position posed by Jesus' criticism. Their status in society

was tied up with the oral tradition. They were honored and revered by the people as righteous, godly men because of their scrupulous observance of its teachings. If the oral tradition collapsed, the Pharisees would fall with it. People whose own welfare and position are bound up with a particular institution generally react with anger and hostility when that institution is criticized.

But Jesus was unaffected by the Pharisees' reaction. He responded: "Every plant which my heavenly Father has not planted will be rooted up" (15:13). He did not believe that the oral tradition was from God. He was confident, therefore, that it could not stand. He believed in God. He believed that God was in charge, and he was convinced that only what God willed would have permanent value.

IV. A Ministry to Gentiles (Matt. 15:21-39)

Jesus withdraws to the region of Tyre and Sidon, where he heals a Gentile woman's daughter who is possessed of a demon. A great crowd, numbering four thousand men with women and children, flocks to him. He feeds them miraculously with seven loaves and a few fish.

1. The healing of a Gentile.   Possibly this unusual excursion by Jesus into Gentile territory was caused by opposition from his enemies, the religious leaders. Tyre and Sidon were cities of ancient Phoenicia to the north of Galilee. The territory was at that time a part of Syria.

Jesus was approached by a woman whom Matthew calls a Canaanite. Canaanites were the ancient inhabitants of Palestine, the foes of the Israelites when they entered the land under the leadership of Joshua. Mark describes the woman in more contemporary terms as a Greek, that is, a Greek-speaking person, and a Syrophoenician, that is, an inhabitant of ancient Phoenicia then a part of Syria (Mark 7:26).

This woman asked Jesus to heal her demon-possessed daughter. The exact nature of the child's problem is not given. The attitude of Jesus toward the woman expressed in his action and his words has always been a problem for Christians. Why did Jesus not respond immediately and affirmatively to the pleas of the poor woman?

There is an often suggested solution to the problem that may be correct. According to it, Jesus acted as he did in an effort to teach the disciples a lesson.

The woman approached Jesus, calling him Son of David which was a title for Messiah. Jesus did not respond, but the disciples did. We can draw the conclusion that Jesus remained silent in order to see what the disciples would say. Their response shows their prejudice and impatience. They had no time for this Gentile woman, nor did they have any compassion for her in her need. They begged Jesus to send her away.

Jesus' answer is difficult: "I was sent only to the lost sheep of the house of Israel." Now we know that Jesus perceived of his mission as being, primarily at least, to Israel. Early Christians believed that Jews were the initial objects of God's redemptive efforts. But many of them believed that his purpose was not limited to the Jews. The gospel had to begin somewhere. A foundation had to be laid. But it was universal in its scope, destined eventually to move from its Jewish beginning to encompass all men.

Let us remember that in this instance Jesus' statement is made to the disciples, not to the woman. Did he intend to test them by it? Was he waiting to see if they understood something of the universality of the gospel? Whatever he may have expected, no reply from them is recorded.

Despite the disciples' evident irritation, the woman persisted: "Lord, help me." Jesus' reply to her is also difficult. There are places in Jewish literature where pagans are called dogs. Was this a true expression of Jesus' attitude toward Gentiles?

Many interpreters have noted that the word used by Jesus is literally "little dogs," that is, puppies. Some people believe that Jesus' statement was made in a somewhat playful fashion.

Still others have concluded that Jesus was testing the faith of the woman. Would she be deterred if he treated her as a Jew might be expected to treat a Gentile?

Whatever the purpose of Jesus, the woman replied with wit and courage. Her daughter's welfare was at stake. Her reply in effect was: "I am not asking for the children's food. All I want is a crumb." We may assume that in the first century, as in the twentieth, people fed their dogs scraps from the table.

The difficulties with Jesus' words recede into the background when we remember his activity—he healed the woman's demon-possessed daughter. Further, he recognized the greatness of the woman's faith. A short time before that he had addressed his own disciple Peter as a man of little faith; to this Gentile woman he exclaims: "Great is your faith!"

2. *The feeding of the multitude.*   The story of the feeding of the crowds here is very much like the narrative of the earlier feeding in chapter 14. It differs in a few minor details as, for example, the size of the multitude. Here four thousand men in addition to women and children are fed.

This large group of people, however, is largely made up of Gentiles. This is brought out in verse 31, which describes their reaction to Jesus' miracles of healing. It says that "they glorified the God of Israel," which implies that they were not Israelites.

The character of the crowd indicates the purpose of the miracle. What Jesus did for the Jews, he also does for the Gentiles. He is their Savior, too.

At the conclusion of the story we are told that Jesus got into a boat and went to the region of Magadan. The location of this place is unknown to us.

V. The Demand for a Sign (Matt. 16:1-4)

Pharisees and Sadducees demand a sign from Jesus. He upbraids them for their failure to interpret the signs of the times, and he leaves them.

1. The request of the religious leaders. Representatives of the two leading Jewish parties, the Pharisees and Sadducees, appear together for the first time since 3:7. Although widely divergent in their other views, they were united in their opposition to Jesus. They made the same request made by the scribes and Pharisees in 12:38. The only difference is that in this passage their motive is specified—they intended to test Jesus. This implies that their request for a sign was not honestly motivated. They hoped to discredit Jesus in the eyes of the people.

2. The response of Jesus. As in the previous instance (12:38), Jesus would not meet the demand for miracles. He would not prove himself on his enemies' terms. Indeed, he consistently refused to perform miracles on request.

Instead he upbraided them for their blindness. They were alert to the signals of nature, but they were impervious to the signs of God. That is, they refused to recognize that they were living in the times when God's sovereign authority was being exercised by his Messiah. They did not need additional signs. What they needed was the forthrightness and openness which would enable them to be sensitive to what God had already done in their midst.

The decisive sign would not be the kind they demanded. Rather, it would be the sign of Jonah (already discussed in connection with 12:39). We are told that Jesus then "left them and departed." This was his answer—withdrawal from them. If men will not receive the God who comes to them in his own way and accept the revelation which he himself gives them, he has no choice but to withdraw. He cannot allow men to determine his program.

13.
You Are the Christ

16:5 to 17:13

I. The Leaven of the Pharisees and Sadducees (Matt. 16: 5-12)

Jesus warns his disciples against the leaven of the religious leaders. Initially they misunderstand his warning. When Jesus explains that he is not talking about bread, they understand that he is warning them against the teachings of the scribes and Pharisees.

1. The meaning of leaven.   Leaven could mean bread. This was the way the disciples initially understood Jesus' statement. In their haste they had neglected to bring food, and they assumed that Jesus was instructing them not to eat the bread of their opponents.

Earlier Jesus used leaven as a symbol of the kingdom of God (Matt. 13:33). Usually, however, it is a metaphor for evil teaching or influence (see 1 Cor. 5:6-8). That is its meaning in this passage.

2. The significance of the teaching.   Leaven works secretly and subtly. Just so, evil influence can corrupt the life of an individual in such a way that he is not aware of it.

The earliest followers of Jesus, living as they did in a society dominated by religious ideas rejected by Jesus, were always in danger of being contaminated and corrupted by those ideas. The temptation to substitute ritual for inward goodness with a resulting self-righteousness was ever present.

It takes concentration and discernment to remain true to the way of life set forth by Jesus. The teachings of Jesus are wholly adequate for his followers and do not need to be supplemented by drawing upon other religious sources. This seems to be the meaning of Jesus' reference to the miraculous feedings. They are symbolic of his teachings which is adequate. The disciples do not need the teachings of the Pharisees and Sadducees.

II. Peter's Confession (Matt. 16:13-21)

Jesus questions his disciples about his identity. Peter confesses that Jesus is the Messiah. Jesus declares to Peter that he will give him the keys to the kingdom with the authority to bind and loose.

1. The importance of the episode. Many scholars have observed that the confession marks a definite turning point in the ministry of Jesus. Prior to this time, Jesus' ministry had been largely a public one as he called the Jewish people to repentance as their appropriate response to the expression of God's rule in his ministry. After the confession Jesus gave more attention to the twelve as he prepared them for the events that lay ahead—events which they did not anticipate.

2. The first question. Jesus retired with his disciples to a region in which he had not been active. It is called the district of Caesarea Philippi. The city lay in the territory under the rule of Philip, a son of Herod the Great. The district of Caesarea Philippi denotes the region under the control of the city.

The question with which Jesus begins his conversation with the disciples is an interesting one. He inquired about the opinions concerning him held by others. In the popular opinion he was one of the great figures of Israel's past come back to life—John the Baptist, Elijah, Jeremiah, or some other great prophet!

It has been popularly supposed that this first question was really preliminary, a way of introducing the important question. The question about the opinion of others is, however, a basic question of tremendous importance to one's own faith. The disciples did not live in a vacuum. They lived in a society where people held

many conflicting opinions about Jesus. They needed to be aware
of the options. They needed to recognize that they had to live
out their own faith among people who did not agree with them.

Mature faith is not a sheltered faith. To the contrary, it is a
faith that is aware of the options. Most Christians will find their
faith tested by opposing and even hostile opinions. They must
be aware of those opinions, must test them, and must be prepared
to be faithful to their convictions when they are a small minority
in the world.

3. The second question. The next question for faith is the
personal one: "But who do you say that I am?" It is not enough
to be knowledgeable about the opinions of others. There comes
a time when one must cease discussing the possibilities and assume
his own stance. Faith requires the courage to assume a position
in the midst of all the conflicting ideas of society.

So the personal question must be faced: Where do I stand?
What is my attitude toward God and the claims made by him
through Jesus?

4. The answer. Peter in his answer went far beyond the popular
opinions. Jesus was much more than a prophet. He was none
other than the Messiah, Israel's long-awaited deliverer. Furthermore, he was a Messiah who transcended human categories. He
was the Son of God, one whose knowledge of God came from
an intimate relationship with him that fitted him to be the unique
revelation of the Father.

This was it! This was the answer which Jesus awaited. "Blessed
are you, Simon Bar-Jona (son of John)," Jesus exulted. Faith's true
answer, as Jesus indicated, comes from no human source. It is
not revealed by "flesh and blood."

Faith is neither irrational nor absurd. It does not contradict
the truth of reason or of nature. But it must go beyond the reach
of human intellect and insight. The knowledge of Jesus' true
identity comes only through revelation. It is an insight given by
the Father.

5. *The beginning of the church.* One may argue convincingly that the church was born on the day of Pentecost. But it was in Peter's confession that the church became a possibility, whenever it was born. At least one person had recognized who Jesus really was, and in this recognition was the beginning of the church.

Jesus gave to Simon a new name. That new name was *Petros* or "Rock." We transliterate it as "Peter," but we should translate it. He was Simon Rock.

Admittedly Peter is not the foundation of the church in the ultimate sense. As Paul recognized, the genuine foundation of the church is Jesus himself (1 Cor. 3:11). But Peter was the foundation in that he was the beginning of the church in a human sense. He was the first who perceived, however dimly, who Jesus was. He was the first to make the confession which all Christians have made in one form or another since that beginning.

Once one human being had responded as Peter responded Jesus could begin to build his church. Peter's faith, as we shall see, was very immature and weak. But at least it was a beginning point.

The word *church*, which appears in none of the other Gospels, must be understood against the background of the Old Testament. It is the *qahal*, "the congregation" or "the people of the Lord." What Jesus will build is not altogether new. It is continuous with the people of God of the past. There is, however, something new. This will be the people of God who belong to and serve him. They constitute *his* church.

This new Israel, the people of God in Christ, had such a tenuous beginning—in the confession of one man acting as the spokesman for only twelve men. But Jesus declared that it was invincible and eternal: "The powers of death (literally, 'the gates of Hades') shall not prevail against it."

Hades is translated as "death" in the RSV. It is the realm of the dead, so the translation is a good one. The metaphor of the gate leads us to think of the abode of the dead as a city. But it is a city powerless to imprison the church. As Christ rose from the dead, so will the church emerge as a victor over death.

6. *The keys of the kingdom.* In this passage Jesus is quoted as giving the keys of the kingdom to Peter. Keys are a symbol of authority. In this case the authority is the transcendent, for the keys belong to the kingdom (the rule) of God.

In the Greek text it is clear that Jesus is speaking to Peter alone. "You" in verse 19 is singular. In a related passage, however, the same authority is granted to the church as a whole (see Matt. 18:15-18). Therefore, it is wrong to think of Peter as possessing a unique authority which was not shared with others.

The authority which Jesus gave to Peter (and the church) is described in the words which follow. It is the authority to "bind" and "loose." These two words represent two Aramaic words found in rabbinic literature. Those words may be translated "forbid" and "permit." They describe the decision of a teacher of the law who declares an action "forbidden" (bound) or "permitted" (loosed). They were also used to describe the imposition of a ban (exclusion from the community) or the lifting of a ban (reconciliation with the community).

It is in this last sense that they should probably be understood in our passage. Neither the apostles nor later church leaders and members exercised the function of deciding whether specific acts were forbidden or permitted. Jesus was not instituting a new legalism to replace the old.

Peter and all those who have come after him were proclaimers of the gospel. Their authority is to be understood in gospel terms. It is the gospel that brings redemption and reconciliation. The church acts to receive those whom God has forgiven and also to restore to its fellowship those erring brothers who are brought to repentance by the power of the gospel. The church's unique responsibility and privilege is to receive those whom God has received. The church does not dictate to heaven, that is, to God. The church's action and God's action are simultaneous. The Spirit of God who moves in the sinner to bring him to confession moves also in the church to cause it to welcome him as a brother. In this way, whatever is done on earth will be done in heaven.

But the gospel is a two-edged sword. It brings reconciliation and forgiveness. But it is also met with hostility and rejection. It is the duty of the proclaimer of the gospel to "bind," that is, to pronounce God's judgment on the unrepentant sinner.

III. The Way of the Cross (Matt. 16:21-28)

Jesus tells his disciples that he must die. When Peter refuses to accept this idea, Jesus rebukes him. He teaches his followers that they must also be willing to lose their lives for his sake.

1. The suffering Messiah. Peter had confessed Jesus as the Messiah. The term, however, was understood by him in a narrow, nationalistic way. He expected Jesus to be the conquering hero who would deliver the Jews from Roman domination.

We see from this passage that faith must be always open to correction. Mature faith is a growing faith. Peter had used the right terminology in his confession, but his understanding of God's purpose in Jesus was very limited.

The confession, however, gives Jesus something to work with. It is only a starting point, as all confessions are. But at least it is that. Once Peter had made the confession that Jesus was Messiah, Jesus could begin to correct the messianic notions of his disciples. He would be a suffering Messiah. His path to glory had to go by the way of the cross.

Peter was unable to accept this notion. It went against everything he had been taught to believe. One moment he was filled with excitement and joy as he contemplated following the glorious Messiah to victory. In the next moment he is bewildered by Jesus' words about suffering and death.

Jesus' response to Peter was sharp and severe: "Get behind me, Satan." We remember that Satan in the temptations attempted to persuade Jesus to take the sensational approach to messiahship. Now Peter, as an instrument of Satan, is putting the same kind of pressure on Jesus.

Instead of being a help, Peter was a "hindrance" or a "stumbling block" (KJV). He represented an attempt to cause Jesus to stumble and fall into the sin of rebelling against God.

2. Suffering and discipleship. Not only must the disciples confess Jesus as the Messiah and understand God's purpose for his life to involve suffering and death. They must also be willing to follow him to the cross, disregarding all concern for their personal safety and welfare. This is the final step in mature faith. It must lead a person to be willing to die if his commitment to the Christ demands it.

The Greek word for disciple means "learner," but this is an inadequate definition of a Christian disciple. For a Christian the term must be defined in the light of passages such as this. Jesus did not call on his disciples to study; he demanded that they follow him. The test of discipleship is not intellectual orthodoxy. It is rather the commitment which we make and live by to follow Jesus, no matter what the cost.

Jesus lays down the law that operates in human existence. The person who attempts to save his own life by cowardly withdrawing from the fray, by seeking the safe and secure position, or by avoiding the hatred that is inevitably directed toward genuine followers of Jesus, will find his attempts frustrated. He may find ease and comfort for a few years, but in the end his efforts will be futile. He will die. The person, however, who takes the risk involved in following Jesus and scorns the false refuges of this world will, paradoxically, find his life. The only trustworthy guarantor of life is God, for only he has power to overcome death.

Jesus points out the futility and folly of seeking security in this world. A man may be so successful in this search that he gains control of the whole world; but even this will not overcome his mortality. He will face death. He has given his life for wealth and power. Now the question arises: Can he give any of that back in exchange for his life? The answer is obvious. Most men of affluence would be willing to trade their empires at the moment of death to buy back the life spent in gaining them. But the world's wealth and power cannot purchase life. Life is a gift from God to those who trust him.

The man, therefore, who has spent his life foolishly must confront the Son of man in judgment. He must answer for his rejection of God and his idolatry.

3. *A difficult saying.* We find in verse 28 a statement by Jesus similar to one already discussed in Matthew 10:23. What was said there is also pertinent here. The "coming of the Son of man" must be understood in some way other than his appearance at the end-time. It is a manifestation of his kingly power in an event which took place in the lives of the disciples. We can only guess what that event is. Perhaps it is the transfiguration, which follows immediately, or the resurrection.

IV. The Transfiguration (Matt. 17:1-13)

Jesus takes Peter, James, and John up a mountain where he is transfigured before them. There he talks with Elijah and Moses. A voice from a cloud repeats the baptismal affirmation: Jesus is the Son of God. In answer to the disciples' question about Elijah, Jesus indicates that John the Baptist had fulfilled the role of Elijah in Jewish messianic expectations.

1. *The relation to the confession.* The transfiguration follows closely on the confession of Jesus as the Messiah and his prediction about his suffering and death. The two episodes are connected by the time reference "after six days." Jesus had taught that suffering was an inescapable part of his destiny. The transfiguration teaches, however, that the suffering Messiah will be exalted ultimately.

2. *The witnesses.* Peter, James, and John seem to have consti-

tuted an inner circle of the twelve. They were the ones chosen by Jesus to accompany him during his agony in Gethsemane (Matt. 26:37). Jesus probably perceived that they were more sensitive to his teaching and had a greater capacity for understanding what he was doing than the other disciples.

These three men were given the privilege of really seeing Jesus as his real identity was projected visibly for a brief time. To this point his true identity had been veiled. When people looked at him, his appearance was no different from that of a thousand other Galileans. But the disciples were able to see him for a moment as "the Lord of glory" (1 Cor. 2:8).

For the disciples the transfiguration was both assurance and call. The assurance was that the way Jesus had taken would lead to glory. The call was for them to follow him. So a fleeting glimpse of his heavenly splendor, a fragile vision in the night, was the only proof given to them that following Jesus in self-renunciation and death leads to participation in glory.

That is what the disciples had to balance against the "solid facts" of the "real world." And so it has always been. On the one side is the allure of what men can count, feel, possess now—a bank account, a luxurious home, social acceptability. On the other side, there is the vision in the night, the gleam of a reality seen all too briefly that summons men to renounce all in dedicating their lives to the service of God and man.

3. Moses and Elijah.   Three commonly accepted ideas about Moses and Elijah may explain why they were appropriate companions of Jesus during the transfiguration. In the Old Testament we read that Elijah did not die but was taken directly to heaven (2 Kings 2:11). According to Jewish tradition, Moses was also assumed into heaven. These two heavenly visitors conversed with Jesus who would also ascend into heaven.

Moreover, Moses was the representative of the law, and Elijah represented the prophets. Their association with Jesus may underline the teaching that Jesus was the fulfillment of the law and the prophets.

Also, both of these Old Testament figures were associated with the messianic age. In Deuteronomy 18:15 we read: "The Lord your God will raise up for you a prophet like me from among you, from your brethren—him you shall heed." Elijah was the expected forerunner of the Messiah (Mal. 4:5). The appearance of Moses and Elijah with Jesus may be intended to confirm the fact that he was the prophet spoken of in Deuteronomy and the Messiah who was to be preceded by Elijah.

4. Peter's reaction. Peter is generally the spokesman for the disciples. Sometimes what he said was right; more often it was wrong.

Apparently Peter jumped to the conclusion that the end of the age had arrived and that the prophecy of Zechariah 14:16-19 was about to be fulfilled. The prophet had declared that all the nations would go up to Jerusalem and participate in the Feast of Booths or Tabernacles. Peter was ready to start getting the booths ready for the celebration of the impending victorious reign of Jesus as the Messiah. This indicates how fleeting was the impression made by Jesus' statements just a week earlier.

5. The voice from the cloud. The cloud represents the She-kinah, the bright cloud which indicated God's visible presence. The cloud "overshadowed" the disciples in the same way that a cloud had rested on the tabernacle when it was filled with God's glory (Ex. 40:34-38).

The voice from the cloud is the voice of God. It repeats the statement made at the baptism. There is, however, an additional remark: "Listen to him," which probably refers to the passage in Deuteronomy cited above (18:15).

At this critical juncture, when Jesus is beginning to teach his disciples about the necessity of his suffering and death, God reaffirms that Jesus is indeed the Son of his good pleasure. Also, he admonishes the disciples to heed his teaching, which contradicts their own traditional notions about how God's Messiah is to act.

6. Jesus' Elijah.   On the descent from the mountain the disciples questioned Jesus about the teaching of the scribes concerning Elijah. Their question is prompted by the appearance of Elijah in the vision of glory. Jesus assures them that his Elijah has already appeared only to be rejected. Men "did not know him," that is, they did not recognize him for what he really was, the forerunner of the Messiah. As men did not recognize John, so they will not recognize Jesus.

14.
The Little Ones

17:14 to 18:35

I. Lessons on Faith and Freedom (Matt. 17:14-27)

Upon his return from the mount of transfiguration Jesus heals an epileptic whom the disciples had not been able to help. He tells them that their problem is lack of faith. Then he makes the second pronouncement to the disciples about his impending suffering. Finally he teaches that neither he nor the disciples are obligated to pay the Temple tax. He instructs Peter, however, to pay it in order not to give offense to the Jews.

1. The healing of the epileptic. In the mission described in chapter 10 the disciples were given authority to heal, but there is no actual description there or elsewhere in the Gospels of a healing miracle performed by the disciples. In this unique story the disciples fail to heal a boy who is an epileptic. The identification of the disease as epilepsy in the RSV and other modern versions is based on its characteristics described here and in Mark 9:18.

It may be that the story is a parallel to the experience of Moses with the Israelites after he had descended from the mountain on which he received the law (Ex. 32). The parallel is not complete, for the Israelites were guilty of idolatry whereas the disciples had only failed to heal a child. Jesus reacted to the disciples' failure, however, by calling them a "faithless and perverse generation," the very words used to describe Israelites in Deuteronomy 32:5.

In New Testament times a miracle of healing was the only hope that such a poor victim had. In our day a Christian father who has an epileptic son will ask his fellow Christians to pray for him. He will usually also take advantage of the marvels of modern medicine which can cure epileptics or at least help them to control their problem. In any case, if healing comes, he will rightfully thank God for his blessing.

2. *The place of faith in miracles of healing.* In the New Testament there is no consistent pattern of the role of faith in miracles of healing. On occasions faith does not seem to be a factor at all in the actual healing (e.g., John 9:1-7; Matt. 8:14-15). In at least one case the faith belongs to the men who bring a sick person to Jesus (Matt. 9:2). In this episode, however, the lack of faith on the part of the disciples is the key to their failure.

Jesus told them that if they possessed faith "as a grain of mustard seed" they would be able to remove mountains.

"Mountains" is used metaphorically. As various commentators have said, if we want to remove actual mountains, we use earth-moving machinery and not prayer. Mountains represent obstacles which can be overcome through faith.

A grain of mustard seed was proverbial as a metaphor for smallness. So Jesus' words should be interpreted to mean that genuine faith, however small, is essential to overcoming obstacles. It is not necessary to have great faith; but the presence of faith in even the smallest amount is indispensable.

What lessons are we to draw from a story like this? First of all, we must assume that people will get sick and die, no matter how much faith Christians have. So the failure of a person for whom we pray to recover is not to be attributed in every case to a lack of faith. On the other hand, we must recognize that God can use us only if we have some faith. It may seem redundant to say it like this, but God can only use us as believers if we are in fact believers.

3. *A question about the payment of the Temple tax.* A poll

tax of a half shekel for each Israelite is required in Exodus 30:11-16. It was imposed on all free male Jews who attained the age of twenty.

In the episode under consideration, Jesus is shown to teach two things. First, he and his disciples are not obligated to pay the tax. Their relation to God exempts them from this obligation. Jesus uses an analogy from contemporary society. Kings did not exact tribute from their sons. In the case of the Roman Empire, the sons would be Roman citizens. Only conquered people had to pay tribute. Neither do the sons of God's kingdom have to pay the dues imposed by the Old Testament.

In the second place, Jesus teaches that his followers are not to misuse their freedom. Out of concern for their fellow Jews, in order not to offend them, the tax will be paid.

Peter is instructed to catch a fish, open his mouth, find there the money for the tax, and pay it. Some interpreters have suggested that this does not imply a miracle. They conclude that Jesus intended Peter to sell the fish and acquire the money for the tax in this way. Jesus' instructions, however, seem to presuppose a miracle. But the emphasis is not on the miracle. It is not even described. The episode was written in order to instruct Jewish followers of Jesus not to abuse their freedom.

The problem is analogous to the kinds of problems faced by Christians in every society and age. Just how far are we to go in expressing our independence of the ideas and practices of the society in which we live? Certainly we are to be sensitive to the problem, refraining from unnecessarily offending persons whom we hope to influence for the gospel.

II. The Importance of "Little Ones" (Matt. 18:1-14)

Jesus answers the question: "Who is the greatest in the kingdom? It is the person who humbles himself like a child. He warns against offending "little ones" and gives advice about dealing with temptations in one's personal life.

1. The greatest in the kingdom.   The disciples' question about
the greatest in the kingdom was a natural one in the context
of their society. In order to conduct one's self properly in social
relations, it was essential to be able to rank people according
to their importance. Apparently the disciples had not yet worked
out an order of social importance and were asking Jesus to help
them to do so.

Jesus' answer was surprising and revolutionary. The child was
the picture of greatness in the kingdom. Children were normally
thought of as the least in importance in a society in which increasing age brought increasing respect.

In essence, Jesus indicated that the standards of the kingdom
reversed the traditional standards of society. In the kingdom those
considered last in society would be the first. Furthermore, his
teachings imply that the disciples were not to get involved in
striving for importance. They were to become children.

The child is used various times as a symbol for the kind of
disciple Jesus wanted. He demanded that his followers become
like children. In fact, only by so doing would they be able to
enter the kingdom at all. Perhaps this is the major implication
of his teaching.

What does it mean to "humble" one's self like a child? The
child is a good figure for a kingdom person because he is totally
dependent. If he is to survive at all, he must depend on his parents
for food, clothing, and care. He cannot provide for himself.

This is the basic idea in humility. The humble person recognizes
his absolute dependence upon God. His security and his future
depend on the love and care of his Father. The greatest disciple,
therefore, is not the proud man who is always comparing his
talents and accomplishments with those of his brothers to their
disadvantage. The greatest disciple is the one who is most aware
of his limitations and contingencies, who is most aware that
everything he has is given, and who is acutely conscious that
he has a future only because God guarantees it.

2. Receiving little ones. In some sayings of Jesus the child also represents the small, weak, unimportant persons in the Christian community. Jesus wanted his followers to care for them.

Men customarily are glad to receive persons of importance. We do not have to be Christians to welcome and honor rulers, rich men, or talented persons. Almost all people are anxious to have men like that visit them. A good illustration of this is what usually happens when the President of the country visits a church.

But the most honored guest of all should be the unimportant, unnoticed people. Jesus said: "Whoever receives one such child in my name receives me." When we welcome a person like this, recognizing his importance because he belongs to our Lord, we are assured that we welcome the Lord himself into our fellowship.

3. Offending little ones. It is a terrible thing to cause a little one to fall into sin. The little one is by definition weak and vulnerable. He looks to others for leadership. To be a leader involves a special responsibility, for his actions may damage those who come under his influence.

Jesus recognized that temptations to sin are inevitable. Temptation translates a word (*skandalon*) which denoted the trigger of a trap over which an animal stumbled and was consequently imprisoned. It is used often in the New Testament to denote that which causes a person to stumble and fall into sin.

The person who is guilty of leading a weak, dependent person into sin or of causing him to sin in any way bears a terrible responsibility. Jesus illustrates just how heinous such an offense is. It would be better if a millstone were fastened around his neck and he were drowned in the sea. The kind of millstone mentioned here is the large heavy kind that had to be turned by an animal. It would be better for a person to die, therefore, than to be the occasion for a little one's turning from the faith.

Verses 8-9 deal with the problem of temptation and sin in the personal life. They are a repetition of Jesus' teaching in Matthew 5:29-30 (see the comments there).

4. The importance of little ones to God. God has a special concern for little ones. That is why it is so serious to despise one of them. "Their angels always behold the face" of the heavenly Father. These may be guardian angels. In Daniel 10:13 each nation has an angel. In Revelation 1:20 God speaks to the churches through their angels. In Acts 12:15 the disciples think that Rhoda has seen Peter's angel.

Whatever the understanding of angel, the truth is clear. The little ones are under God's watchful, caring eye. And he notices any slight, offense, or sin against them.

The care of God for the least of the disciples is illustrated by the parable of the lost sheep. It is found in another context in Luke (15:3-7). Here it tells us about the value that God places on the "little ones." They are not important to society. They have neither wealth, power, nor influence. What do they matter? The answer is: not very much to men, but a great deal to God.

The shepherd may have a hundred sheep. If one of them is lost, however, he does not console himself with the fact that he still has ninety-nine. He does not say: "The one who was lost is small and weak. So it really doesn't matter." Indeed, it is likely that the lost sheep will be the one who is unable to keep up with the flock. The shepherd's concern, nevertheless, forces him out to look for and find the sheep.

This is a picture of the immeasurable concern of God for his people. It should also be a picture of the concern which believers have for every member of the flock.

III. Teachings on Forgiveness (Matt. 18:15-35)

Jesus gives instructions for dealing with problems of fellowship. Every effort is to be used to effect a reconciliation with the offending brother. If he refuses to respond to those efforts, he is to be excluded from the fellowship. If he asks forgiveness, he is to be forgiven. The parable of the two debtors illustrates God's judgment on unforgiveness.

1. Who takes the initiative? Jesus taught in the Sermon on the Mount (5:23-26) that the person who offends his brother has the responsibility for taking the initiative to restore fellowship with him. Although we do not always follow this pattern, it seems reasonable to us. But what are we to do when our brother offends us? We might suppose that the responsibility rests on him to make amends. Surprisingly, however, Jesus does not take that position. He says that the responsibility still rests upon us.

I am always responsible for attempting to repair the break in fellowship with my brother, no matter who is to blame. The genuine Christian is always pained when there is a barrier between him and his brother. He knows that the will of his Lord is that the community be united in love for one another. Furthermore, he knows that, as a peacemaker, he is in the business of reconciliation and that he cannot shift the responsibility for effecting it to someone else by any logic or argument.

2. The purpose of discipline. This passage is about church discipline. Unfortunately, the word discipline has harsh connotations. We generally take it to mean punishment for a person who commits a wrong. But discipline in the Christian community is always positive. It does not aim at punishment but at the restoration of the erring brother.

Our motive for talking to an erring brother makes all the difference in the world in our treatment of him. If our desire is revenge or if we want to punish him for his wrongs, we shall hardly be able to win him. The whole purpose of the method proposed in Jesus' teaching is to gain the brother. To the genuine Christian his own personal injury or embarrassment is secondary. The real pain is caused by the loss of fellowship with his brother. His real purpose is not personal reparation but the joy of fellowship with his brother.

3. The method of discipline. Jesus proposes a plan which involves three progressive steps. The offended individual goes first to the offender. If he is not successful in his personal efforts at reconciliation, he is to go a second time with other members of the community as witnesses. The responsibility of these witnesses is not only to attest to the reaction of the guilty party. They also witness about the attempts of the offended person to make reconciliation. That is, they can verify whether he has gone to the brother in a hard, demanding, or vengeful way or whether he has made a truly Christian effort to be reconciled with him.

Finally, if all else fails, the problem is to be brought to the church where the last effort to deal with it is to be made. Should the offending person fail to respond to the efforts to bring him back into fellowship, he is to become as a "Gentile and tax collector" to the church. That is, he is to have the same relation to the church that Gentiles and tax collectors had to the Jewish community. In other words, he is to be excluded.

It is not so much, however, that the community excludes him. He is in reality not a part of it because he willfully and perversely refuses to deal with the barrier that exists between him and his brother. A member of the New Testament church was not a person who had his name on the church roll. He was rather a member of a family, a vital part of a community. One can have his name on the roll of the church but at the same time be isolated from the life of the community because there is no genuine relationship between him and his brothers.

4. *The authority of the church.*   We dealt with the matter of binding and loosing in connection with Matthew 16:19. There this authority was given to Peter. Here, however, we see that it is church authority. The only concrete illustration about its use is the example of dealing with problems in relationships.

According to this and related passages, the church does have authority to receive and expel members. But this is not arbitrary authority. Many churches have violated it by receiving people on other than a gospel basis, that is, on other than faith in Jesus Christ as Savior and Lord.

Many other churches have violated their authority by rejection or expelling people on other than a gospel basis. People have been rejected because the color of their skin was wrong. They have also been expelled because they refused to conform to cultural norms that had little or no connection with the gospel.

The church has the privilege and responsibility of accepting all persons whom God accepts. It also has the responsibility for dealing with problems in their fellowship. In this case, it is charged with excluding those whose hardened rejection of Christian love and refusal to seek forgiveness separate them from the community. That is, the body of believers have warrant for excluding only the people who first exclude them. The church's actions conform to heaven's (God's) actions only if this pattern is followed.

5. Guidance for the church. The church, however, not only has a pattern to follow. Jesus also promises help from God in decision-making of the kind described in the passage. The church can pray to God for guidance.

There is a condition to be met, however, without which the church cannot have the assurance that God will answer their plea for help. At least two must agree on the matter about which prayer is made.

At first glance the statement of Jesus may seem to lead to an unwarranted conclusion. Does the unanimous vote of the church determine God's action? No. Verse 20 points the way to the true interpretation of the promise. The agreement is one that is produced by divine guidance. Agreement is possible because Jesus through the Spirit is in the midst of the church. The responsibility of the church is not to decide what it wants to do. It is rather to discover what her Lord wishes and then to ask God to help accomplish his will.

6. Teachings about forgiveness. Peter's question in verse 21 is a logical one. How often can one be expected to forgive the person who offends him? Shall he forgive him seven times? This is the number Jesus himself uses in Luke 17:4. Seven is the number of completion and can stand for an unlimited number of times.

In the Matthean passage, however, Jesus makes it clear that the disciple is to set no limits on forgiveness: he should forgive seventy times seven. The number of times he forgives is determined by the number of occasions on which his brother asks forgiveness. Every time he seeks forgiveness, it must be granted.

The parable of the two debtors shows how serious it is for a disciple to withhold forgiveness from his brother. The first man in the story owes his king an enormous sum—ten thousand talents. In the margin of the RSV a talent is given the estimated worth of a thousand dollars. The debt was so huge that the poor man could not hope to pay it. The only thing that could save him was the leniency of his creditor. Amazingly, the king does just that, for no reason except his compassion for the helpless fellow.

One would think that such an experience would cause the man to have a generous, forgiving attitude toward the whole world. But such was not the case. As the man leaves the presence of the king, he meets a fellow servant who owes him a hundred denarii. The RSV says the denarius was worth twenty cents. The sum was insignificant compared to the large debt of which the man had been forgiven. He does not treat his fellow servant as he has just been treated. He is harsh and unforgiving. When the king hears about his treatment of the fellow servant, he reverses his decision and gives the man the same treatment that he had accorded his debtor.

The lesson is clear. Man stands in relation to God as a debtor. He is helpless to pay his debt, so his only hope is that God will forgive him. God does forgive us. But God's forgiveness, if it is accepted and becomes the basis of our hope, is creative. It expresses itself in our willingness to forgive people who sin against us. The person who is truly forgiven by God is aware of this and acts accordingly. After all, our brother's sin against us is paltry when compared to our sin against God. It is always true that a harsh, unforgiving spirit is a sure sign that an individual does not know what it means to be forgiven by God.

15.
Who Can Be Saved?

19:1 to 20:16

I. Teachings on Marriage and Divorce (Matt. 19:1-12)

Jesus leaves Galilee and begins the journey to Jerusalem. The Pharisees ask him about divorce. Jesus replies that God's will for marriage is indissoluble union between a man and his wife. Divorce was allowed in the law because of human weakness. The disciples say that under this condition it is better not to marry. Jesus teaches that some people may indeed choose to remain single for the sake of the kingdom.

1. The question about divorce. This encounter with the Pharisees is placed in "Judea beyond the Jordan." This is a loose designation, for properly speaking Judea in its entirety lay to the west of the Jordan. Perea, which was under the rule of Herod Antipas, lay to the west of the Jordan.

The question "Is it lawful to divorce one's wife for any cause?" was debated among the Pharisees. In Deuteronomy 24:1 we read that a man may divorce his wife "if she finds no favor in his eyes because he has found some indecency in her." The school which followed the great rabbi Hillel gave a liberal interpretation to that statement, holding that a man could divorce his wife for almost "any cause." The rival school of Shammai was more conservative and held that the only grounds for divorce was adultery on the part of the wife.

2. Jesus' answer. Much of Jesus' answer is a repetition of the passage found in Matthew 5:31-32 (see comments there). There are, however, some additional ideas in this passage.

161

In his remarks about marriage Jesus calls attention to God's purpose as expressed at "the beginning," that is, at the time of creation. When he created man and woman, God declared that they should be one (literally "one flesh," as in the KJV). They were no longer independent, autonomous individuals but they formed a union which God intended to be indissoluble.

The beginning was the time when all creation functioned in harmony under the will of God. It was common Jewish belief that the end would be as the beginning. God would vanquish evil and bring the rebellious forces of the universe under his rule. Jesus taught that the situation of the end had come upon the disciples. They had been brought under the rule of God. Therefore, the ideal for them was the pattern set forth at the beginning, when God had created the universe and sin had not yet entered the picture. In this situation there was no place for divorce. Divorce is an expression of the disharmony, conflict, and failure that result from rebellion against God's rule.

Jesus' attitude toward the provision for divorce in the law is interesting and instructive. It gives us a clue for understanding the Old Testament. Jesus believed that the Old Testament was from God. Nevertheless, he did not believe that it was to be accepted blindly and without reservation as a norm for the life of his disciples. Much of the Old Testament, as we saw in our discussion of the Sermon on the Mount, did not measure up to the higher principles laid down by Jesus for his followers.

Therefore, Jesus interpreted the statute on divorce as provisional. It was an accommodation to the human situation and took into account man's limitations as a sinner. It did not, however, express God's ultimate, highest will for man. That was expressed at the beginning, before sin was a factor.

We, as Christians, hold that the Old Testament must be interpreted in the light of the incarnation. We have clear precedent for this in the teaching of Jesus. Our insight about God begins with the revelation of God himself in Jesus Christ. Anything that falls below this revelation must be understood as not expressing God's highest will for Christian disciples, even if it is found in the Old Testament.

3. The disciples' reaction. Jesus' followers were well aware of the possible problems in marriage. For many people it would be impossible to live up to the ideal of an indissoluble union. Perhaps the best course would be never to marry. Then one would not have to be concerned about the possibility of failure in marriage.

The option of celibacy, however, is not without its problems. As Jesus said, not all men can receive this "precept." It is better to translate the word as "saying" rather than "precept." It refers either to the preceding disciples' comment (v. 10) or to Jesus' own statement that follows (v. 12). In either case, it seems to mean that not all men can remain single.

There are some men, of course, who have no need to marry. They were born without the capacity to function sexually. Others had been made eunuchs by men. Kings often had men emasculated who were to be given positions of trust in their affairs.

Others chose not to marry "for the sake of the kingdom." John the Baptist was one of these. Jesus also did not marry, and apparently neither did Paul. The key phrase is "for the sake of the kingdom." The celibate life is not intrinsically better than the married life. Indeed, we could make a good case for the opposite point of view.

The rule of God, nevertheless, must take precedence over all else. If marriage is a hindrance to the work to which God has called a person, he should be willing to make this sacrifice. The question probably should be resolved on this basis: Is the work to which God has called me going to make it impossible to fulfill my moral responsibilities to a wife and children?

II. How to Have Eternal Life (Matt. 19:13-30)

When the disciples try to keep some children away from

Jesus, he rebukes them. Jesus says that the kingdom belongs to people who are like children. A rich man asks Jesus what he must do to have eternal life. Jesus asks him to give away his riches and follow him, whereupon the rich man leaves sorrowfully. Jesus talks about how difficult it is for rich people to enter the kingdom but affirms that with God all things are possible. He assures his disciples that anyone who gives up worldly possessions and family to follow him will be rewarded.

1. *The little children.*   Children were brought to Jesus, possibly by their parents, "that he might lay his hands on them and pray." It was a Jewish custom for children to ask their parents to bless them in this way. The disciples attempted to prevent the people from bringing their children to Jesus. Perhaps they thought that Jesus was too busy to give his time to the children. Their efforts, however, were contrary to the teachings of Jesus that we have seen. The disciples are to receive little ones.

When this story is told in the Gospel of Mark (10:13-16), it is said that Jesus became indignant with the disciples. Mark also reports Jesus as saying "whoever does not receive the kingdom of God like a child shall not enter it." Humble dependence upon and trust in God are prerequisite attitudes for entering the kingdom.

2. *The rich man.*   The story about the rich man stands in contrast to the story about the children. Jesus taught that it was necessary to "receive the kingdom," that is, accept the rule of God. God's salvation is freely given and must be humbly received; it cannot be earned or purchased.

The rich man's question shows how far he was from understanding the basic requirement of the kingdom. "What good deed must I do," he asks, "to have eternal life?" He believed that salvation was something one must earn by good works.

First of all, Jesus questions the man's use of the adjective "good." In Mark the man also addresses Jesus as "good teacher." People today, like the rich man, often use words loosely. Jesus tells him that good can be applied properly only to God. All else is tainted by imperfections, limitation, and sin.

Jesus in his reply goes along with the rich man's own religious ideas: "If you would enter life, keep the commandments." In reply to the request for more specific information, Jesus cites some of the Ten Commandments which deal with human relations. He adds to them the saying from Leviticus 19:18, "You shall love your neighbor as yourself."

The reply of the rich man was probably expected by Jesus. The man had faithfully observed all those commandments in accordance with the way they were interpreted in the pharisaic circles. In spite of his efforts he was not confident that he had done everything God might require of him. He felt that Jesus might be able to point out something that he was still failing to do. So he asked: "What do I still lack?"

Jesus went in through the back door, so to speak: "Sell what you possess and give to the poor, and you will have treasure in heaven; and come, follow me." Jesus was asking him to do the one thing he could not bring himself to do. If he had not possessed so much, perhaps he could have done it. But he possessed great wealth. To his credit, he was saddened as he went away. He knew that Jesus had touched on the one great weakness of his life. He understood the truth of the judgment of Jesus, but he could not bring himself to live by it.

What was the man's problem? The answer is clear. He was an idolater. He was violating the First Commandment. His money was his god. He valued his possessions above all else. They were the source of his security and his hope. He could not bear to divest himself of that security and place himself in a position where God would be his only hope.

Interestingly enough, we have made a cliché out of Jesus' statement to another man: "You must be born again." We quote that to everybody who wants to know how to enter the kingdom.

But we do not cite the words of Jesus to the rich man when we tell people how to enter the kingdom. In our modern affluent society Jesus might tell more of us, "Get rid of your possessions and follow me." If we love anything more than we love God, that thing is our idol. We must get rid of our idols. Otherwise, like the rich man, we have not really followed Jesus.

3. *Riches, a barrier to the kingdom.* Jesus said a lot about possessions. We saw in our comments on Matthew 6:19 ff. that he recognized the basic peril of wealth. It can be a rival to God for men's affections and loyalties. It is very difficult, therefore, for a rich person to enter the kingdom—as difficult as it is for a camel to go through a needle's eye.

Various attempts have been made to attenuate Jesus' saying in Matthew 19:24. For example, it has been suggested that Jesus actually used a word for "rope" which is very similar to the term for "camel." It is about as difficult to pass a rope through a needle's eye, however, as it is to put a camel through it. Others have suggested that the "needle's eye" was a gate. But the saying should be understood literally. Jesus was talking about a real camel and a real needle.

"Who then can be saved?" asks the astonished disciples. They were probably accustomed to thinking of wealth as a sign of blessing from God. If rich people, upon whom God has bestowed such favor, have a problem, can anyone be saved? The answer is: "By his own power, no one. It is impossible. But with God, the impossible is possible. In God's power, any one can be saved." God's power is great enough to change the heart even of an idolatrous rich man. Indeed, the salvation of any person, rich or poor, is a miracle of grace.

4. *Rewards for disciples.* What about those who unlike the rich man have left all to follow Jesus? This question is typical of Peter at this time and is one that he probably would not ask when he reached greater maturity. It certainly does not represent the highest level of Christian thinking.

But Jesus answers the question. The answer is essentially this: God's blessings to believers will be far more than they deserve. The twelve will sit on thrones, judging the twelve tribes of Israel. This means that the disciples will share in Christ's glory and power in "the new world." "The new world" is a translation of a word meaning literally "regeneration" (KJV). Paul also says the saints will judge the world (1 Cor. 6:2). Those who have made sacrifices by giving up family and possessions will receive "a hundred fold," that is, more than they can imagine.

The passage, however, ends with a warning: "Many that are first will be last, and the last first." God's standard of measuring reverses human standards. The very people who think they have done the most and should receive the most will be disappointed. So we need to be careful about our expectations. God's greatest blessings will go to those who least expect them—to the obscure, humble people who do not enjoy the places of honor and prestige, who are not known as the "great Christian leaders."

III. The Parable of the Workers in the Vineyard (Matt. 20: 1-16)

Jesus says that the kingdom of heaven can be compared to the situation of a landowner who hires people to work in his vineyard at different times during the day. At the end of the day, however, he pays all of them, even the ones who worked for only an hour, the same wage.

1. The situation in the parable. The focus of attention in the parable is on the first group and the last one. The first workers were employed early in the morning. In Palestine the work day began at sunrise and ended when the first stars appeared, approximately twelve hours.

Only the first group of workers entered into an agreement with the landowner. They would receive a denarius, worth about twenty cents. A denarius was the normal wage for a day of common labor.

Other workers were found in the marketplace. This was where unemployed laborers congregated, hoping that someone would hire them. At 9:00 A.M. (the third hour), 12:00 noon (the sixth hour), 3:00 P.M. (the ninth hour), and even at 5:00 P.M. one hour before quitting time, the landowner hired groups of these idle workers and sent them into his vineyard. No agreement was made with any men hired later in the day.

At the end of the day the owner ordered the men to be paid. According to the Old Testament (Lev. 19:13; Deut. 24:15), workers were to be paid each day's wages on that day.

Surprisingly, the employer paid those who had worked only an hour for a full day of work. Not surprisingly, the men who had worked all day expected a bonus and became angry. They had worked all day and had borne the scorching heat of the wind that blew off the desert.

The employer rejected their complaint. He had lived up to his bargain with them. He could do what he wished with his own money. They should not "begrudge his generosity," or, literally, "have an evil eye" (KJV), because he is good. The "evil eye" was idiomatic for a stingy, greedy spirit (see on Matt. 6:22-23).

2. *The application of the parable.* The parable was probably told to Jewish legalists. They had driven a bargain with God. They expected God to reward them for their lifelong faithfulness. In their theology, God owed salvation to whoever did good work.

These were the people who particularly resented Jesus' association with sinners. They were infuriated when Jesus taught that God accepted people who had not lived righteous lives. It turned their theology upside down.

But this is exactly Jesus' teaching. Those who came in at the eleventh hour will receive life in the world to come. They will receive it, not because they have earned it, but because God is generous and good.

16.
Behold Your King Is Coming

20:17 to 21:46

I. Nearing Jerusalem (Matt. 20:17-34)

As Jesus is on his way to Jerusalem he makes the third and last prediction of his suffering and death. The mother of John and James requests places of honor for her sons in the kingdom. Jesus teaches that greatness among the disciples will be measured in terms of service. Jesus heals two blind men outside Jericho.

1. The request for places of honor. Jesus had told his followers at various points that rejection and death awaited him. In this passage he tells them that this tragic fate will occur when they reach Jerusalem. The disciples simply could not believe what he was saying. They had their own ideas about what Jesus was going to do. They anticipated that Jesus was going to overthrow the Romans and begin his messianic rule in Jerusalem (see Luke 19:11).

This false expectation serves as the background for the request made by the mother of James and John. There was evidently a power struggle going on among the disciples, and she wished to gain an advantage for her sons. She asks the future King, therefore, to make a commitment on their behalf. She wants him to issue a decree that her sons will have the places of honor and authority in his kingdom. The places on the right hand and left hand belong to the chief officers of a king.

Jesus, however, brings the conversation back to the reality of the moment. The first question is not whether they will rule with him but whether they will suffer with him. Can they drink of his cup, endure without falling away the bitter experience of suffering and death?

The brash answer comes immediately: "We are able." As events were to show, they did not know what they were talking about. In Jesus' last tragic hours the disciples all deserted him. Looking beyond that moment of failure, however, Jesus affirms: "You will drink my cup." The disciples were unfaithful to Jesus in the hour of his rejection. They fled rather than share his cup of pain. In later years the story was different. They suffered indignity and persecution. Many of them also followed Jesus to a martyr's death. We read, for example, in Acts 12:1-2 that James for whom his mother had requested a position of prestige was put to death by Herod Agrippa I. The disciples did in fact drink of the cup of their Lord's suffering. They eventually passed the severe test.

Jesus went on to say that endurance of suffering would not automatically give them places of honor. Only God had the authority to determine questions of reward and honor. Jesus forces his disciples to have faith in God. They must trust in God for their future, confident that whatever he does will be right.

2. *The standard for greatness.* The text tells us that the rest of the twelve became indignant at the attempts of James and John to gain an advantage over them. They probably were angry because the two apostles had asked for positions that each of the others coveted for himself.

At any rate, the remarks of Jesus about greatness are addressed to the total group. The disciples' problem was that they had been influenced by the structures of pagan society. They were taking their cue from the "rulers of the Gentiles."

In pagan society there was a constant struggle for advantage. When a person succeeded in achieving his ambitions, he used his lofty position to "lord it over" his fellowmen, to order them around, and to demand that they serve him.

Jesus taught that in his society things were different. The usual structure of human society was to be turned upside down. Those attitudes and actions which brought a person fame and power in the world would make a person last in Jesus' community. The servant role, on the other hand, the role that was least desirable in the world, would be the most important role among his followers.

The word for servant is *diakonos*. It was a word used to describe, for example, a person who waited on tables. We transliterate it and use it to identify an office in the church, the office of deacon. But all Christians are "deacons," according to the words of Jesus.

The pattern for the disciple is the example of Jesus himself. He did not come to be served. He spent his life in helping those who might well have been serving him. "Son of man" in this context may mean simply "I" (see the comments on Matt. 9:6).

As a final, climactic act of service Jesus gave his life to help people. "Ransom" is a word that is taken from the master-slave relationship. It is the price paid to redeem a slave and set him free. Jesus saw men as slaves, helpless victims of evil. He came to help them by setting them free, even though the price of their liberation was crucifixion.

The words of Jesus judge our so-called Christian organizations. Are those organizations characterized by a grasping for honor and position? We must admit, sadly, that such is too often the case.

3. *The healing of two blind men.* The city of Jericho lay about fifteen miles northeast of Jerusalem. New Testament Jericho was built by Herod the Great to serve as his winter capital. As Jesus was leaving this important city, he was met by two blind men who appealed to him for an act of mercy, addressing him by the title "Son of David."

The blind men were rebuked by the crowd. Was it because they considered the blind men unimportant and impertinent? Or, was it because they used a title which Jews had given to their hoped-for king? It certainly had revolutionary implications for the people who heard it. To call Jesus Messiah in public could bring the wrath of the authorities down upon him.

The attitude of Jesus was in marked contrast with the impatience of the crowd. Jesus stopped in his journey and healed the two men.

II. The Entrance into Jerusalem (Matt. 21:1-11)

Jesus enters Jerusalem, riding on an ass as a proclamation that he comes in peace. He is hailed by the crowds as the Son of David, the messianic King.

1. The manner of Jesus' entrance. Why did Jesus choose this moment to force the Jewish people and authorities to make a decision about him? The evangelists do not speculate about the reason for forcing a crisis at this time. What is clear is that the decisive moment had come for Jesus in his ministry. He presented himself in the Jewish capital as the Messiah. He did so with the full recognition of the choice which the religious leaders would make. They would reject him and destroy him.

By the manner of his entrance Jesus proclaimed the nature of his messiahship. He did not enter as a conquering king riding on a warrior's horse. Instead, he rode into the city on a donkey, the symbol of humility and peace. Matthew understood this to be a fulfilment of the prophecy of Zechariah 9:9.

The location of Bethphage is unknown. It is probably the place from which the donkey was secured. According to Matthew, two animals were brought, an ass and her colt, whereas the other evangelists mention only one.

The instructions in verses 2-3 do not give a clear picture to the modern reader. Is Jesus himself "the Lord" who has need of the ass? In this case, there probably was a prearranged plan for the owner to furnish the animal for Jesus' entrance.

"Lord," however, can also mean "master" or "owner." Some scholars suggest that the owner of the animals was one of the disciples. In this case, the messengers were simply to tell the person in charge of the animals that they were authorized by the owner to get them.

2. *The reaction of the crowd.* The coming of Jesus to Jerusalem produced an overwhelming messianic excitement among the people. The Synoptic Gospels (Matthew, Mark, Luke) tell of this one visit to Jerusalem by Jesus. John, however, apparently describes three visits to the capital. The fact that Jesus was immediately recognized and was the cause of such intense enthusiasm indicates that he was well known to many of the people gathered for the festival.

Even though Jesus rode into Jerusalem on a humble ass, the people gave him a royal welcome. They acclaimed him as their long-awaited king, the Son of David. They welcomed him as one who came "in the name of the Lord," that is, in God's name. They said that he deserved all praise, even from the hosts of heaven "in the highest." The multitudes acclaimed Jesus with a quotation of Psalm 118:26. It was the greeting given to the pilgrims who came to Jerusalem to celebrate the Feast of Tabernacles.

When the triumphal procession entered Jerusalem, the whole city was "stirred." The word is used also to describe the tremors of an earthquake. Some of the people did not know him: "Who is this?" they asked. In the reply Jesus was identified as the prophet from Nazareth and not as Son of David. Evidently people had heard of the "prophet from Nazareth" even if they did not know him personally.

III. Judgment on the Nation (Matt. 21:12-46)

Jesus drives the sellers of sacrificial animals out of the Temple and overturns the tables of the moneychangers. He refuses to quiet the crowds who acclaim him as Messiah. On the second day in Jerusalem, he curses a fruitless fig tree. On entering the Temple he is questioned by the Jewish leaders about the source of his authority. He illustrates rebellion of the Jewish people against God by telling the parables of the two sons and of the wicked farmers.

1. The cleansing of the Temple. The commercial activities which aroused the anger of Jesus took place in the court of the Gentiles, that area of the Temple which Gentiles were permitted to enter. The Jewish people were required to provide unblemished birds and animals for sacrifice in the Temple. It was a convenience to the worshipers to be able to buy these animals at the Temple itself. During the first century the family of Annas (high priest A.D. 6-15) controlled the markets for the sale of sacrificial animals.

During New Testament times, the half-shekel Temple tax had to be paid in Tyrian silver coins. Prior to the Passover, money changers set up tables first in the towns outside Jerusalem and later as the feast drew near in the Temple to make it possible for pilgrims to exchange their foreign currency for the required coins. Jesus was probably protesting against the abuses of the system when he drove out the sellers of animals and overturned the tables of the money changers.

In Malachi 3:1 the prophet tells us that the messenger of the Lord "will suddenly come to his temple." Jesus' action may be thought of as the fulfillment of that prophecy. As the Messiah, he appears in the Temple to cleanse it of evil practices.

Jesus himself quoted from Isaiah 56:7: "My house shall be called a house of prayer." But he says, with a reference from Jeremiah 7:11, "You make it a den of robbers." The exploitation of people by charging exorbitant prices is a sin of stealing just as reprehensible as breaking into their houses to rob them. Today we would call this a "white-collar" crime, because it was part of the system and was committed by the respectable people.

This kind of sin is even more serious when it is committed by religious leaders who use the institutions of religion for personal profiteering. The New Testament teaches that the minister deserves a living. But it also teaches that the use of religion to gain personal wealth is a terrible sin. People who profess to follow

Jesus—the same Jesus who cleansed the Temple—have made God's house a "den of robbers" far too many times.

2. Out of the mouths of babes.   The lame and the blind came to Jesus and he healed them. Jesus, therefore, stands in marked contrast to the priests who exploit the people. He is the Good Shepherd.

As a result of these miracles, the people acclaimed him as Messiah. The chief priests and scribes, however, became indignant at this reaction of the crowds. Evidently they wanted Jesus to put a stop to the demonstrations. But he replied to them by quoting Psalm 8:2. The common, ordinary people, "babes and sucklings," acknowledged Jesus when their leaders refused to do so.

3. The fruitless fig tree.   The miracle described in the story about the cursing of the fig tree has disturbed some readers of the Gospel. It is an act contrary to the general nature of Jesus' miracles. Usually he heals and saves; he does not destroy. In the temptations he refused to use his power to satisfy his own hunger. Here, however, he destroys a tree because it does not have fruit for him to eat.

Another problem arises from the fact that this was the spring of the year, too early for a fig tree to produce edible fruit. This problem is not insurmountable because it was possible for a tree to have an early small crop of edible figs.

What is the meaning of the miracle? Probably in the context of Jesus' ministry in Jerusalem it was an acted pronouncement of judgment on a fruitless nation (cf. Jer. 8:13). God will destroy the nation because it has not produced the desired fruit.

The story also expresses the power of Jesus. The disciples "marveled" when they saw that the tree withered immediately. Also it teaches the importance of faith in prayer (see comments on Matt. 16:20-21).

4. The question of authority.   The Jewish leaders' question about the authority of Jesus was provoked by his actions in taking charge of the Temple. He was not a member of the Sanhedrin.

The council had granted him no authority to correct abuses in the Temple. He was not even an accredited rabbi. What right had he to do what he did?

A question deserves an answer only if it is an honest question. If the inquirer is seeking information, a teacher has a responsibility to give him information. But if a teacher answers a question, he has a right to assume that the seeker will evaluate the information honestly and act sincerely upon it.

One of the best ways to answer a dishonest question, one designed to entrap, is by asking a question. If a person asks you something, you have the right to ask him the same kind of question. Jesus, therefore, responded to his interrogators with a question designed to show their dishonesty in refusing to face up to the issues involved in their question.

The leaders had asked Jesus about his authority. He countered by asking then about the authority of John. Did John's authority come from heaven (from God) or from men? Like Jesus, John stood outside the institutional structures. He was not an ordained or commissioned teacher.

John had based his ministry on a direct commission from God. Either he was correct or his ministry was to be explained solely in human terms. God had called him, or else he had acted on his own initiative. Which was it?

The question was related to Jesus' own ministry. He was in the same situation as John, a nonaccredited teacher. Also, he claimed to be the "Coming One" about whom John had preached, and he had been so recognized by the wilderness prophet. In this sense, Jesus' question was a fair one where the question of the leaders had been a devious one.

The leaders were in an impossible situation and they knew it. If they admitted that John had divine authority, they would answer their own question. Why then had they not believed his pronouncement about Jesus? On the other hand, should they say that John was acting on his own, they would incur the hostility of the people who held John to be a prophet, a spokesman called and commissioned by God himself.

They were forced to say, "We do not know." Their refusal to answer Jesus' question relieved him of the responsibility to answer theirs. Refusing to face the central issue of John's ministry, they were too dishonest to face the issue of Jesus' ministry.

5. *The parable of the two sons.* The two sons represent two groups in Israel. The first son refuses to do what his father wishes but later repents and goes to work in the vineyard. The second talks like a good, obedient son but fails to act like one. He does not fulfill his father's command.

The rebellious son represents the sinners in Israel. The tax collectors and prostitutes were by and large immoral people. They had failed to respect the law of God. But when God acted in the person of John the Baptist, they had repented, turning to God, and, thus, doing his will.

The religious leaders, for their part, had talked like good children of God. But they refused to accept and act on God's message as proclaimed by John the Baptist. Jesus' affirmation must have shocked and infuriated his audience. Tax collectors and prostitutes were the lowest of all sinners on the religious scale. Scribes and Pharisees were the good people, the keepers of the law, God's favorites. How dare Jesus to say that God would prefer immoral outcasts to them?

One of the startling characteristics of Jesus' ministry is that he preached the message of judgment to the righteous and the message of grace to sinners. A disturbing question intrudes itself. Have we Christians largely reversed Jesus' order? Is our preaching more like the approach of the Jewish religious men than like his? Do we not also preach the message of judgment to sinners and the message of grace to the righteous? Such preaching is futile, for the sinners already feel condemned and the righteous already feel they have earned God's grace. We would do well to follow Jesus' example when we preach. We must warn the self-righteous of God's judgment, and we must assure the sinners of God's grace.

6. The parable of the vineyard. This is another parable that expresses God's judgment on the Jewish people. It is related to Isaiah 5:1-5 where God is compared to a farmer who lavishes care on his vineyard. The vineyard represents Israel.

In the parable the moral rights of the owner of the vineyard are based not only upon his ownership but also on the care and work expended on it to ensure its productivity. This is a way of emphasizing God's relationship to Israel. He was Israel's God. Not only so, he had done everything that could be done to ensure its productivity.

The servants in the story represent the prophets of the Old Testament. They had been sent to claim the fruits for God by calling the people to serve and love him. Consistently, however, they had been mistreated.

The crowning insult is the way the tenants treat the son. By killing him they will be able to claim the vineyard for themselves. This, of course, is the sin of the crucifixion. God is excluded from the vineyard which is his. He is pushed out of his world. The crucifixion is the ultimate act of rebellion against God, a declaration of autonomy by men. By rejecting the Son, men reject the Father and take possession of what does not belong to them.

But God can use even man's rejection to accomplish his purpose. The stone that is rejected as unfit by human builders of their own kingdom becomes the beginning of a new building that will honor God.

Nor is God tied to one nation. If these people reject him, God will create a new people. This saying of Jesus looks toward the creation of the church out of Gentiles.

The chief priests and Pharisees understood the parable of Jesus and were driven to murderous fury by it. They wanted to kill Jesus but did not have the courage to do so because Jesus was so popular.

17.
Why Put Me to the Test?

22:1-46

I. The Parable of the Wedding Feast (Matt. 22:1-14)

Jesus compares the kingdom of heaven to the situation of a king who plans a wedding for his son. The story is divided into three parts. In the first part (vv. 2-7) the guests who are invited first reject the invitation and are punished. Next, an invitation goes out to the people in the streets (vv. 8-10), and the wedding hall is filled with guests who were not chosen for their station or class. When the king makes his appearance at the wedding party, he excludes a guest who is improperly clothed (vv. 11-14).

1. The first invitation. A wedding was a very important function in ancient society. The wedding of the king's son and heir was exceptionally significant, a time of national rejoicing and celebration. The story probably is based on familiar custom. The prospective guests were given an invitation. Later when preparations for the event were completed the summons to attend was sent out.

There is a most unusual development in the story told by Jesus. When the first summons is sent out, the invited guests refuse to respond. Another chance is given when other servants are dispatched to repeat the invitation. No earthly king would do that. But God is incredibly patient. His invitation goes out again and yet again.

The reaction of the people who are invited is a comment on the relationship between God and Israel. Jesus has been proclaim-

179

ing the inbreaking of the kingdom of God, calling men to repent
and accept the rule of their King. He has sent his own messengers
out to call the people to turn to God.

These efforts have met with various responses. Some have gone
on with life as if nothing were happening. The pressing affairs
of business and property claim their attention. They do not have
time to attend to the invitation of the king. They treat his summons
with indifference.

Others, however, have reacted with hostility. The preceding
passage (21:45-46) tells about the desire of the religious leaders
to arrest Jesus. The king's reaction to the hostility of his subjects
is predictable. In such circumstances a ruler would punish his
subjects unmercifully for such disrespect. Jesus teaches that God's
call cannot be ignored with impunity. Who is man to set himself
arrogantly against the invitation sent out by the Sovereign Ruler
of the universe?

2. *The new invitation.*   The king's plans will not be frustrated
by such shabby treatment. There will be a response. The wedding
will take place. The wedding hall will be filled.

Jesus taught that God's redemptive purposes cannot be frustrated by man's hardness of heart and rebellion. Too many people
arrogantly presumed that they were essential to God's plan. They
thought that God could not exclude them without failing in his
promises—but they were wrong, very wrong. God does not exclude
men—they exclude themselves by refusing to heed his gracious
invitation. But when they exclude themselves, God will continue
to do his work.

Religion itself can be one of the most effective barriers to a
genuine sensitivity to God's call. Any person or group of people
who believe that they are indispensable to God have by that
attitude placed themselves in a position of alienation from God.

The place of the first guests is taken by people "both good
and bad" from the streets. This heterogeneous crowd represents
the tax gatherers and sinners who had responded to the invitation

of Jesus which the leaders had rejected. In the time of Matthew's Gospel "the good and bad" people may have been the Gentiles who were entering the church in increasing numbers.

3. The king's appearance. At the height of the festivities the king made his appearance at the wedding hall. One of the guests stood out from the rest; he was inappropriately dressed for the occasion.

God's call goes out indiscriminately: "Many are called." Acceptance, nevertheless, is not indiscriminate. "Few are chosen." The invited must present themselves appropriately. Tax gatherers, sinners, and prostitutes were recipients of God's gracious invitation. Nevertheless, they must appear in proper dress. Although God is gracious to sinners, he is not insensitive to morality. He is not a kind of "grandfather in the sky" who indulgently overlooks man's evil. His invitation to the outcasts, underprivileged, and scorned, implies a responsibility. From them also he demands a changed direction and a commitment to live according to his will.

The man who misunderstood the king's generous invitation was excluded from the festival. He was thrown into outer darkness. In ancient cities the contrast was great between a lighted festival hall and the unrelieved darkness outside. There the excluded man could "weep and gnash his teeth" in frustration and regret for his cavalier attitude.

II. God and Caesar (Matt. 22:15-22)

Disciples of the Pharisees along with Herodians ask Jesus if it is lawful to pay tax to Caesar. Jesus tells them to give to Caesar what belongs to him and to God what belongs to him.

1. The situation. The question of the annual poll tax demanded by the Roman government from conquered people under its direct rule was an explosive one. The census taken in A.D. 6 for the purpose of levying the tax precipitated a revolt of some Jews led by Judas of Galilee. Anyone who advocated paying the tax would incur the wrath of the more radical elements of the population, such as the Zealots.

Two groups teamed up in an unlikely alliance to ask Jesus the question about taxes. Pharisees sent some of their lesser figures, that is, their "disciples." They were accompanied by Herodians, Jewish supporters of the rule of the Herods under Roman domination. They would be sure to report any radical statement made by Jesus to the proper authorities. On the other hand, the Pharisees would publish abroad any statement from him that seemed to support Roman rule.

The purpose of the group was clearly to put Jesus in a dilemma, or to "test" him. The question was one of those for which there was no answer that would satisfy everybody.

2. *Jesus' answer.*   Why did Jesus ask for the coin (in Greek, a denarius)? Was it because he did not have one, as many have suggested? Perhaps he wanted to emphasize graphically that his interrogators carried such coins with them. At any rate, a coin was produced. "Whose likeness and inscription is this?" Jesus asked. "Caesar's" was the reply. The ruling Caesar at that time was Tiberius (A.D. 14-37).

The point was clear to the listeners. In ancient times one of the responsibilities of the ruler was the minting and circulation of coins to facilitate commerce in his realm. The money thus circulated really belonged to the ruler. The acceptance and use of that coin by the people in his kingdom was tantamount to their recognition of his sovereignty.

In those circumstances the answer to the question about taxes was unequivocal. It was a matter of basic morality. If you have something that belongs to another and he requests it, you must give it back to him. Those men had coins that actually belonged to Caesar. If Caesar asked for them, they had but one choice. "Give back (a literal translation of the verb) to Caesar what belongs to him."

The men had asked Jesus about their duty to Caesar, but Jesus was far more concerned with the rule of God. By carrying coins with Caesar's image, those Jewish leaders were violating their own teachings about idolatry. In their effort to avoid making "graven images," Jews avoided images of all kinds. According to current standards, therefore, the men were guilty of an idolatrous practice.

"Give back to God what belongs to him." One must return Caesar's coins upon demand, but there was to be no worship of the emperor. The supreme King was God and to him men owed their ultimate allegiance.

3. The application.   A tremendous superstructure of theories about the separation of church and state has been built upon the meager foundation of Jesus' statement. One thing is clear. Jesus did not stand with the radical revolutionaries of the Jewish nation. He was no zealot who advocated the forcible overthrow of Roman rule.

To read back into Jesus' statement modern theories about church and state, however, is an anachronism of the worst sort. Jesus certainly placed limitations upon Caesar's rights. But the reverse is not true. He placed no limitation on God's right to rule in every sphere of human existence including the social and political. This is the weakness in the approach of many people in our times. They not only limit Caesar, which is right. They also limit God, which is incredible.

Jewish people, including Jesus, had no theory of separation of church and state. For them ideally all of life was under God's rule.

The point is this: The believer is always under the rule of God in all his actions. When he acts in the political or social realm, he acts as a Christian. The first and most important question for him is never about the will of the state. It is always about the will of God.

In modern society it is essential that church and state as

institutions not usurp functions that do not belong to them. But it is extremely wrong for a believer to divide his life into various spheres. God has something to say about everything his children do.

III. Encounter with the Sadducees (Matt. 22:23-33)

In an attempt to ridicule belief in the resurrection, some Sadducees present a hypothetical case to Jesus. A woman has been married successively to seven brothers. Whose wife will she be in the resurrection? Jesus replies that they have a false notion of God's power and a wrong interpretation of their Scriptures.

1. The situation. As we have noted elsewhere (see comments on Matt. 3:7), the Pharisees and Sadducees differed sharply on certain issues. Two important differences must be understood as the background for interpreting this passage. The Sadducees accepted only the Pentateuch, the first five Old Testament books, as Scripture. They also rejected the oral traditions of the Pharisees, where ideas about the resurrection were elaborated. They claimed that the doctrine of the resurrection was not taught in the law.

Jesus was more in sympathy theologically with Pharisees than with Sadducees. He embraced the Pharisaic position on the resurrection which the Sadducees attempted to ridicule by their hypothetical example.

The so-called "law of levirate marriage," which furnishes the background of the Sadducees' question, is found in Deuteronomy 25:5-6. According to this law, if a man died leaving a childless widow, his brother was obliged to marry her. Any child of such a marriage was considered the heir of the dead brother. The purpose of the law was to assure that the deceased would have an heir.

2. Jesus' answer. Jesus critized the Sadducaic position on two counts. First of all, their theology underestimated the power of God. They assumed that in the resurrection life would be identical with what we know now. Jesus taught, however, that life in the resurrection would be transformed by God. Heavenly society will not be characterized by exactly the kind of human relationships which we experience now. All earthly categories will be transcended and men will be like "angels." Among angels there is no marriage nor giving in marriage.

In the second place, Jesus challenged the Sadducees on the basis of their interpretation of Scripture. Interestingly he did not challenge their view of Scripture.

Too often we attempt to meet questions and criticisms by attacking the character or beliefs of people who disagree with us. Jesus, however, sought to deal with the issue on the Sadducees' own terms. Belief in the Pentateuch was common ground on which both stood.

His quotation (v. 32) is from the Pentateuch (Ex. 3:6,16) which the Sadducees accepted as authoritative. God calls himself the God of Abraham, Isaac, and Jacob. All three of these men had died. Did the Sadducees actually think that the Lord would characterize himself as the God of dead men? His point is clear: these men now live in the presence of God.

IV. Encounter with Pharisees (Matt. 22:34-46)

This passage tells of two exchanges between Jesus and the Pharisees. In the first, a lawyer asks Jesus about the great commandment in the law. In the second, Jesus calls into question their view of the Messiah as son of David, since David in a psalm called him Lord.

1. The great commandment. The rabbis engaged in numerous attempts to define the heart of the law. They also had many discussions about the "weightiest" or greatest of the Commandments. This kind of theological debate furnishes the background for the question put to Jesus: "Which is the greatest Commandment in the law?" We are told that a lawyer asked the question.

A lawyer was an expert in Old Testament law.

It is not clear how such a question would put Jesus to a test. Perhaps his opponents hoped to get him involved in theological controversy. Possibly he would take a position that would detract from his stature in the eyes of some of the people.

Jesus replied with a summary of the law that brought together two verses of Scripture (Deut. 6:5 and Lev. 19:18). There is not one great commandment, there are two which are closely related: love for God and love for neighbor.

Jesus added an additional word. All of God's will, expressed not only in the law but also in the prophets, depends on these two commandments. If a man truly loves God with all his being and his neighbor as himself, he will not need additional command- ments. He will do in everything exactly what God wants him to do.

Paul with Jesus perceived that true morality does not come from obedience to an outward code (Gal. 5:14). It arises out of an inward commitment rather than out of an outward compulsion. No man is truly good if he is good only out of fear. The person whom you can trust to retain his integrity in times of moral testing is the man who loves God fully and who loves his neighbor as himself.

2. Love for self.   Christian people have generally felt that self-love is wrong. Of course, a certain kind of self-love is wrong. When we try to exalt ourselves at the expense of others, when we try to get ahead by walking on others, we are sinners. This is not genuine self-love, however. Arrogance and disregard for others generally stem from a basic insecurity. They are, surpris- ingly, indications of self-hatred.

What is genuine love for the self? It is a sense of one's own dignity and worth as a human being based upon the biblical concept of man. It is, in other words, self-respect.

A genuine appreciation of our own worth is the basis for our appreciation of the worth of all other men. A person who has true self-respect will have respect for others. An individual who knows his own value does not have to prove himself by pushing other people down.

3. The question about David's son. One of the tenets of Jewish messianic expectation was that the Messiah would fulfill the prophecy in 2 Samuel 7:12-16. He would be the son who would reestablish the hegemony of David's line in Jerusalem and rule over a restored Israel.

Jesus' exchange with the Pharisees in verses 41-46 implies that he considered this expectation inadequate and limited. Was the Messiah really David's son? If so why do we find the statement in one of the Davidic psalms: "The Lord [i.e., God] said to my Lord [i.e., the Messiah], sit at my right hand?"

No, the Messiah is not really David's son. He is much more exalted than that. He is really David's Lord.

His place of rule will not be an earthly throne in Jerusalem. He will rule from the right hand of God, a position of preeminent power and glory. The narrow, nationalistic view of the Jewish people was totally inadequate. The limited, earthly view of Messiah's rule was far short of the mark.

18.
Woe to You, Scribes and Pharisees

23:1-39

I. Criticism of Religious Leaders (Matt. 23:1-12)

Jesus criticizes scribes and Pharisees because they do not practice what they preach, because of their unfeeling attitude toward people, and because of their ostentation.

1. Teaching and practice. The scribes were the learned doctors of the law, responsible for its application to the contemporary life of the people and for its transmission. They were distinct from but closely related to Pharisees. A Pharisee was characterized by his devotion to the oral tradition, but he was not necessarily an accredited legal expert or teacher. A scribe was not necessarily a Pharisee, but it is probable that most of them belonged to that sect.

Moses' seat was probably the chair in the synagogue reserved for the authoritative teacher of the law in a Jewish community. From this position they expounded the meaning of the law to the worshipers. We may get the idea that Jesus was opposed to all Pharisaic teachings. Such was not the case. To the contrary, many of Jesus' own beliefs were identical with Pharisaic positions. He was opposed to what he considered to be contradictory to a prophetic understanding of the Old Testament. But he would have agreed with much that he heard of Pharisaic expositions of the law. Insofar as the teachers proclaimed what God intended in the law, they were to be heeded.

The problem was, however, that some of them did not apply their teachings to their own lives. There was a discernible difference between profession and practice.

This is a genuine danger to religious teachers and preachers in any age. The sin of hypocrisy is a constant pitfall. One reason for this is that it is much easier to talk about God's will than it is to do it.

2. A callous attitude toward people. Jesus accused the religious leaders of binding heavy burdens and laying them on men's shoulders. "Bind" may have to do with the rulings about what was permitted or forbidden to people under the law (see comments on Matt. 16:19).

One of the main distinctions between Jesus' approach to religion and that of other teachers is seen right here. Jesus was concerned primarily with God and people. The personal element was at the very heart of his understanding of religion. The religious leaders were concerned primarily about institutions and rules. By multiplying the rules that governed every aspect of daily life, they placed a heavy burden on people.

To the religious leaders, rules were important for their own sake; what is more significant, they were more important than people. When rules become more important than people, religion becomes a burden and constitutes a barrier to doing God's will.

The unfeeling attitude of the leaders was seen in their lack of compassion. No matter how much the rules damaged human beings or made their life more difficult, the leaders did not "move them with their finger." That is, they did not make the least effort to mitigate the burden of religion out of concern for individuals.

The truth that we Christians must see is that Pharisaism is a tendency of our religion as well as of the Jewish religion. We must guard against the tendency of making institutions, programs, and rules more important than people.

3. Love for display. The problems that Jesus talked about were not just Jewish problems or Pharisaic problems. They were human problems, caused by sin. Men loved to move ahead of their neighbors. Jesus saw a lot of vying and scrambling for the places of honor. These were the places nearest the host at the table. He saw the religious leaders competing for the best seats in the synagogue. He also noticed how they loved public recognition, the ceremonious public greetings accorded to the most esteemed people.

The title "rabbi" was just coming into use in the first century. It was an honorific title for scholars which meant "my Lord" or "my great one." The love for titles is a common human trait. A title sets its bearer apart from the common herd as someone special. The love for titles arises out of our sinful desire to be considered better than our fellowmen.

Christian disciples are not to be characterized by this drive for recognition. No disciple is to seek honor and prestige at the expense of his brother. Titles are the product of a pagan society where men strive for superiority over their fellows. Christian disciples constitute a different kind of fellowship—a community of brothers who all share equally in the life of the family of God.

Modern equivalents of "rabbi" are "professor" and "doctor." The New Testament shows clearly that certain members of the community are given the gift of "teaching." What is at issue here is not the gift or function of teaching. What is at issue is the title of "teacher." Jesus does teach an important lesson: the teacher is not to be set apart from his brothers. All Christians have their own functions which are as essential to the life of the community as that of the teachers.

The elevation of a few to places of honor and prestige always has an unwholesome effect on the rest. They tend to think of themselves as less worthy, less important to the life of the community. The community becomes divided and structured in ways that resemble pagan society. This is contrary to God's will for his people.

Christ is the teacher or master. All others are learners. God is Father, all others are children. The only appropriate title for

Christians to use of one another is "brother" or "sister."

The principle of Christ operates in his community. The person who exalts himself at the expense of his brothers will be humbled by God. God is going to turn our pagan structures upside down— the structures that prevail in our conventions, institutions, and schools. The people who are considered by God to be the greatest are the obscure humble folk who faithfully minister in Christ's name with no selfish thought for personal reward.

II. Woes on Religious Leaders (Matt. 23:13-33)

In a series of seven woes Jesus condemns the scribes and Pharisees for their sins.

1. First woe: shutting the kingdom. The legal experts of Judaism had made entrance into the kingdom difficult. God would justify the man who kept the law, they taught. They had built a fence around the law with their traditions in order to protect it and assure that it would not be broken. Therefore, it was not a matter only of keeping the law. It was essential to keep it in the way they had interpreted it.

For vast numbers of people, keeping those traditions was next to impossible. These were the "sinners" or "the people of the land." They were not always scrupulous about observing the purification rites, nor could they be. They did not have the time nor the opportunity even to learn all the provisions in the traditions.

According to the religious leaders, such people were "sinners," outside the pale. They were not in the kingdom. And, as is usually the case, these people accepted the verdict of their religious leaders.

According to Jesus, not only did the leaders bar the entrance to the kingdom to others. They themselves had not entered. They prided themselves on their subjection to the rule of God. Of one thing we can be sure. The person who takes pride in his status before God does not in fact enjoy such a position. Acceptance by institutional religion based on conformity to institutional requirements is not equivalent to acceptance by God.

2. Second woe: the failure of their missionary efforts. Judaism of the first century was a missionary religion. Many of its adherents were zealous in their efforts to convert pagans to Judaism. The results of their efforts were significant. Many Gentiles were becoming proselytes. A non-Jew became a proselyte by submitting to circumcision, if he was a male, by baptism (probably), and by offering a sacrifice in the Temple.

But Jesus characterized the converts as "twice as much child of hell" as were the missionaries. This means that the converts were apt to be even more bigoted, narrow, and arrogant than people born into Judaism. It is often true that the converts to a movement become even more fanatic than the original members of the movement.

3. Third woe: their teachings about oaths. The taking of an oath was regarded in the Old Testament as a serious matter. As a guarantee that they would keep their word or fulfill their contract, men would often vow to do so in the name of God. Various passages in the law emphasized the necessity of keeping such oaths and the sin of failing to do so (Lev. 19:12; Num. 30:2; Deut. 23:21).

Men, being the sinners that they are, attempted to avoid the risk inherent in failing to keep their vows to God by swearing on lesser things. The rabbis found it necessary in these circumstances to render decisions about which of these popular oaths were binding.

Jesus, however, scornfully rejected all such splitting of hairs. Swearing by the altar is just as serious as swearing by the gift which is on it, if not more so. One could argue, as Jesus did, that the altar was greater than the gift or that the Temple was greater than the gold which adorned it.

From Jesus' point of view all oaths were equally binding. Man was responsible before God to keep any oath or vow that he took. Indeed, as we have seen (Matt. 5:33-37), Jesus considered all oaths superfluous in a society of honest men. The simple, unadorned word of a man of integrity is just as binding to him as any oath he might take.

4. Fourth woe: their concern with trifles. The tithing (a tenth) of wine, grain, oil, fruit, flocks, and herds was prescribed in the Old Testament (Lev. 27:30; Deut. 14:22). The scribes had amplified this to include even the herbs grown in the garden. Mint, dill, and cummin were herbs used for seasoning. Dill and cummin were also used for medicinal purposes. The tithing of these herbs is an example of the "fence around the law." The interpretation of the law extended the perimeter around it so that there was no possibility of infringing on the law itself. That is, you did more than the law itself required to be on the safe side.

Jesus had no quarrel with their practice of tithing: "These things you ought to have done."

But these practices were trivial compared to the really important things or "weightier matters." But the God revealed in Jesus is not concerned about trivia. He is concerned about justice. He wants people to do right. He is concerned about mercy. He leads people to be actively involved in helping those who are in desperate need. He is concerned about faith. If this is the correct translation, it refers to the trust of men in God. The word, however, can be translated "faithfulness." In this case it refers to the persevering commitment to living according to God's will.

The problem about excessive attention to trivia is that people miss what is really significant. Many religious people in Jesus' day were guilty of this. Sadly enough, many persons in our own time are equally guilty.

5. Fifth woe: their concern for outward piety rather than inward purity. Ceremonial purity was extremely important to the people who lived by the scribal interpretation of the law. Failure to wash the hands before eating or the dishes out of which one ate was a sin (see Mark 7:2-4; John 2:6). Cleanliness is a recommended practice for good health, but people in the first century knew nothing of germs. The Jewish people followed the rules because of religious sanctions. It was a part of the effort to be right before God. Whether or not you eat out of a dirty dish, however, has nothing to do with your relationship to God.

According to Jesus, religious people had put the emphasis on the wrong place. They cleansed their hands on the outside, but inside their hearts were full of extortion and greed. This may be understood in two ways. Perhaps the plate and the cup were symbolic of the person. They were very careful about outward ceremonial purity, but they were dirty on the inside. They took advantage of other people and exploited them economically, which showed that they were filled with rapacity, that is, unrestrained desire or greed.

There is another possible understanding of Jesus' statement. They cleansed the outside of the cup and the plate, but they filled the inside with the fruits of exploitation and greed. Once again we see that Jesus emphasized God's demand for an inward unselfishness and love which manifests itself in generosity toward others.

6. *The sixth woe: their hypocrisy.*   One problem with legalism is that it results in hypocrisy. The focus of attention is on the outward display of religiosity. The purpose is to conform to a set of commonly agreed upon rules. This creates a contradiction between what a man really is on the inside and what he appears to be on the outside.

Originally in Greek drama "hypocrite" was the act of playing a part or the person who played a part. That is what a legalist is. He is playing a part written for him by the religious community.

Only when the motivation for outward goodness comes from within can this contradiction be overcome. The person who is genuinely good on the inside will express his goodness in his attitudes and acts. He is pained that his actions fall short of what he really desires. So the good man is probably never known by others to be as good as he really is.

Jesus said the hypocrites were like whitewashed tombs. A month before Passover, tombs were whitewashed so that they could be seen clearly. The purpose was to prevent people from coming into contact with graves accidentally. They believed that contact with a tomb was religiously defiling. The purpose of whitewashing the tombs was not to beautify them, but this was the result. Jesus seized on the contrast. Outside the tombs were beautiful and looked pure. Within, however, were the evidences of death—bones or decaying bodies. Jesus said that hypocrites were like that.

7. *The seventh woe: they honor dead prophets but persecute living ones.* The lot of the prophet is always a difficult one. They challenge the evils of the status quo. People in power are the ones who profit from the status quo, and they have the resources to punish prophets who threaten their position. In the history of Israel the tragic fate of the prophets is an expression of the nation's rebellion against God. When a prophet speaks, people have three options: they can repent and change, they can ignore the prophet, or they can kill him. More often than not Israel had responded in the last way.

But a strange thing happens after prophets are dead and buried. Succeeding generations honor them, eulogize them, and make their tombs national shrines. That is exactly what Israel had done. But our attitude toward prophets is shown by the way we treat living ones and not by the honor we heap on dead ones.

Jesus' contemporaries recognized that the men who killed the prophets were their "fathers." Jesus affirmed that they were right; they were in truth the sons of those men. The statement is loaded with irony. To be a son of someone means to have his character. Not only were they the physical descendants of the prophets' murderers. They were like them in character. They rejected and killed contemporary prophets.

"Fill up the measure of your fathers" is a taunt. It means "complete the work that your fathers began." The atrocities described in verse 34 probably point to the persecution of Christian prophets, God's spokesmen in the first century.

As murderers of contemporary prophets, the enemies of the gospel would share the guilt of their fathers. All the "righteous blood shed on earth" would come upon them.

III. A Threat and a Lament (Matt. 23:34-39)

Jesus predicts that his people will reject his messengers in the way that they had rejected the ones God had sent to them in the past. Because of this they will suffer. He expresses sorrow over the impending destruction of Jerusalem which will be a consequence of their rebellion.

1. The threat.   Jesus predicts that the Jewish people will continue the pattern of rejecting the messengers of God. He will send "prophets, wise men, and scribes" to them, and they will be treated harshly. They will be killed, crucified, scourged, and persecuted. Crucifixion was a sentence imposed by Romans but not adopted by Jews. Scourging was a common punishment meted out by local synagogue courts. The maximum number of lashes permitted in such penalities was 39 (cf. 2 Cor. 11:24).

Jesus had tried to turn the Jewish people from the mad course of rebellion against Rome. He had tried to get them to accept a different understanding of the rule of God and the role of his Messiah. They had failed to respond to his efforts. The inevitable result was the collapse of the Judean state and the destruction of Jerusalem in A.D. 70.

In a sense, the people of that generation paid a price for the sins of the men who had shed innocent blood from Abel to Zechariah. Abel was the first martyr in the Bible. The last one mentioned in the Hebrew Old Testament was Zechariah. His murder is recorded in 2 Chronicles 24:20-22. Second Chronicles is the last book in the Hebrew Bible which has a different order from our Old Testament. This Zechariah's father was Jehoida. The Barachiah mentioned by Matthew was the father of the prophet Zechariah.

It may seem unfair that one generation must pay for the sins of its forebears. Yet we know that this is a fact of history. How many of the critical problems of our own country are the result of sins and errors of our own fathers? The practice of slavery is just one of these.

2. The lament. The knowledge that Jerusalem will be destroyed fills Jesus with great sorrow. He would have saved them this fate. He would have protected them as a hen does her threatened chicks. His redemptive efforts have been rejected. As a result, Israel's "house is forsaken and desolate." The house is the Temple, and it is desolate because God is withdrawing his presence from it.

Jesus declared solemnly and sadly: "You will not see me again, until you say, "Blessed be he who comes in the name of the Lord." With these sad and prophetic words Jesus brings his mission to Israel to a close in the Gospel of Matthew. He has tried and failed. Now he faces rejection. However, he will return in glory.

19.
Take Heed that
No One Leads You Astray

24:1-51

I. Warning Against Being Misled (Matt. 24:1-14)

Jesus predicts the destruction of the Temple. His disciples ask him about the signs of the end. He warns them not to be misled by false proclamations of his coming. Neither disasters, such as wars and earthquakes, nor severe persecution mean that the end is at hand. The gospel must be preached to the nations before the end comes.

1. The disciples' questions. Herod the great began what amounted to a reconstruction of the second Temple in 19 B.C. This third Temple, a complex of buildings covering some thirteen acres of Mount Moriah, may not have been completely finished at the outbreak of the first Jewish-Roman war in A.D. 66. Josephus informs us that the Temple was constructed of massive blocks of white marble, which from a distance looked like a gleaming, snowcapped mountain peak. It was ornamented with gold, precious stones, and costly tapestries and was one of the wonders of the first-century world.

The disciples admiringly pointed out the buildings of the Temple. Jesus replied with a prediction that the imposing edifice, which possessed such an air of permanency, would one day be reduced to rubble. In A.D. 70 the Romans put the Temple to the torch and subsequently under Caesar's orders leveled its walls in their demolition of the city. When they had finished, the place where Israel's proud capital once stood was an uninhabited wasteland. Just as Jeremiah had foreseen the destruction of the first

Temple as the result of Judah's disastrous foreign policy (Jer. 26:6), so Jesus anticipated that Herod's Temple would be destroyed.

The disciples' questions tie together the destruction of the Temple, the coming of the Lord, and the end of the age. In other words, the destruction of the Temple is one of the signs of the end-time in this point of view.

2. Jesus' answer.   Evidently there were Christians who saw in the destruction of the Temple an indication that the end of the age was at hand. The words of Jesus are directed first of all to this false assumption. When the Temple is destroyed, pretenders will take advantage of the hopes and beliefs of Christian people and declare themselves to be the Messiah.

Jesus cautioned his followers not to be misled by such demagogues. They were not to associate the destruction of the Temple with the end of the world and were to reject all persons who made false claims on this basis.

3. Suffering and persecution.   Times of severe suffering have traditionally been eras which spawn false hopes of the end. Perhaps this is natural. In the midst of the horrors of war the forces of evil seem to reach an intolerable climax, and the future appears bleak and hopeless. People may then conclude that this is a situation that can only be solved by a divine intervention. Surely the moment when evil seems to have gained absolute supremacy is an opportune one for God to manifest his sovereign power and gain the ultimate victory.

During severe persecutions, Christians are apt to long for a transcendent solution to their problem. When evil pervades the power structure and Christians are hopeless victims of that power, can God long delay his answer to their prayer: "Maranatha, come, Lord Jesus"?

Under such conditions hopeless people are often gullible victims of men who preach with assurance that the end is at hand. The signs are right. God will soon intervene to save his own and punish the doers of evil.

Jesus taught, however, that those tragic, widespread disasters are not the signs of the end. He warned: "Many false prophets will arise and lead many astray." They are only "the beginning of the sufferings." The truth is that as far back as history records them, the world has suffered from famines, earthquakes, and wars.

Times of suffering will heighten the hope of many. But it will also have the opposite effect on others: "Most men's love will grow cold." The failure of God to act to alleviate suffering and establish his rule will cause men to lose heart. In such circumstances the fainthearted will never persevere. So Jesus promises: "He who endures to the end will be saved" (see comment on Matt. 10:22).

Verse 14 is a very interesting verse. It expresses an idea that is found elsewhere in the New Testament (Acts 1:6-8 for example). The time between the incarnation and the end of history is the time of the world mission of the church.

This present age is given its meaning by its being an integral part in the history of redemption. It is the time for the gospel to be preached to all men. From some people we could get the idea that life for the believer is simply a matter of waiting for the Lord to come. From this point of view life in the present is a sort of vacuum, robbed of its real meaning.

That, however, is not a correct Christian view of this age. God is at work. He has a purpose in history as it continues. It is this redemptive purpose which gives us a clue to the meaning of our lives. Believers are not to stand around gazing into heaven, waiting for the Lord to return. They are to understand the present as extremely meaningful and challenging.

The gospel will be preached throughout the world only if believers become actively involved in God's work of redemption. The proper attitude for the Christian is not absorption with the end but commitment to serving God in the present through a witness to the gospel.

II. The Destruction of Jerusalem (Matt. 24:15-28)

Jesus tells about the severe suffering that will take place in the siege of Jerusalem. He warns his followers not to be misled by false claims about the appearance of the Messiah. He assures them that all will know it when the Son of man appears.

1. The desolating sacrilege. The phrase "the desolating sacrilege" is based on references in Daniel (cf. Dan. 11:31: "the abomination that makes desolate"). Scholars generally agree that the phrase in Daniel refers to the altar of Zeus erected by Antiochus Epiphanes on the altar of burnt offering in the Temple. This idolatrous act emptied the Temple (i.e. "made it desolate") of true worshipers and of God himself. Three years later (165 B.C.) the altar was cleansed and sacrifices to God were reinstituted.

For us, the question about the "desolating sacrilege" concerns its meaning in the gospel. Some people see it as a reference to the attempt by the emperor Caligula to set up a statue of himself in the Temple (A.D. 40).

More than likely, however, the "desolating sacrilege" refers to the presence of the victorious Roman army in the Temple area. Indeed, Luke has the phrase "when you see Jerusalem surrounded by armies" instead of "the desolating sacrilege" (Luke 21:20). So it is preferable to understand Jesus' remarks as a reference to the siege of Jerusalem in A.D. 70.

At that moment of crisis Christians are not to remain in Judea. They must "flee to the mountains." In A.D. 70 they escaped to Pella in the Jordan Valley, rather than flee to the mountains.

2. The urgency of the crisis. The situation will be so serious that a person who happens to be on the housetop when the Roman troops appear is not to worry about his possessions in the house. The man who deposited his coat at the edge of the field when he began to work must not return for it. It will be an especially difficult time for pregnant women and nursing mothers who will be hampered in their flight.

If the crisis occurs in the winter, the severe weather will increase the suffering. Any who have scruples about breaking the traditions of travel on the sabbath should pray that the time for flight not occur then. A sabbath day's journey was about three-fifths of a mile.

The only hope for the survival of any Jewish people will be for the slaughter to be stopped somehow. Jesus predicts that there will be survivors for the sake of the elect, that is, Jewish Christians.

3. False messianic hopes.   Jesus saw that false messianic hopes would be raised during the siege of Jerusalem. Men would arise to proclaim that the Messiah had come to save the Jews from the impending disaster and lead them to victory over the Romans. Some would claim that the Messiah was in the wilderness ready to lead his followers. Jesus warned believers not to accept such claims. There was an idea current among the Jews that the Messiah would appear in the wilderness of Judea. This was the reason why the Qumran sectarians established their community in that area, to await the salvation of the Lord.

Others would say that the Messiah was "in the inner rooms." This seems to reflect a belief in a hidden Messiah who was already in the world but had not made his public appearance.

4. The coming of the Son of man.   Jesus' teaching here is clear and important. People were not to give heed to anyone or any group who claimed the Messiah had come. When he did appear, it would not be known to a select few. His coming would be "as the lightning" which is seen by all as it flashes across the sky. Everybody will be aware of his coming at the same time.

The coming of the Son of man would be the time of judgment. A carcass inevitably attracts eagles (perhaps vultures is a better translation). Just so would deeds of evil attract the judgment of God.

III. Signs of the Coming of the Son of Man (Matt. 24: 29-33)

Jesus talks about the signs of the coming of the Son of man. He uses the example of a fig tree. The budding of the tree means that summer is at hand. Just so the appearance of the signs means that the end is near.

1. The coming of the Son of man. The signs of the coming of the Son of man are not natural or historical. That is, neither famines nor earthquakes, neither war nor persecution is a sign of the end. The coming of the Son of man will be preceded by cosmic disasters much more spectacular and miraculous: the sun darkened, the failure of the moon to shine, etc. This is the common language of apocalyptic literature, a kind of writing in vogue at the time.

Jesus also refers to the "sign of the Son of man" which will appear "in heaven." Later Christians came to believe that this sign would be the appearance of the Son of man on the cross with outstretched hands. There is no way of knowing what this sign really is.

At his coming all the tribes of the earth will mourn, as predicted in Zechariah 12:10-14. The Son of man will come on clouds of heaven with power and great glory fulfilling the description in Daniel 7:13-14. The "elect," that is, the saved, will be gathered together by the sound of the trumpet. In Isaiah 27:13 the trumpet assembles the scattered Israelites. In 1 Thessalonians 4:16 the trumpet announces the resurrection of the dead.

2. The sign of the fig tree. One of the major problems facing the interpreter of passages like this is distinguishing between those statements related to the end-time and those related to history, that is, to the siege of Jerusalem. Does the example of the fig tree relate to the signs of the coming of the Son of man just preceding it? Or, does it relate to the national and religious crisis produced by the Jewish-Roman war? One cannot be sure.

It is probably best to understand it in connection with the end, however. The budding of the fig tree means that summer is near. Just so will the cosmic disturbances described in verse 29 announce the imminent end of history. The Greek does not make it clear whether we should translate the phrase "he is near" in verse 33 or "it is near" (as in the KJV). If it is "he is near," the phrase refers to the Son of man. If, however, we translate "it is near," it refers to the destruction of Jerusalem.

IV. The Unpredictable Time of the End (Matt. 24:34-51)

Jesus declares that no one except the Father knows the time of the end. It will come upon men unexpectedly as they are involved in the daily routine of life. When the end does come, God's judgment will cut across social relations. Men must always be prepared because the Son of man will come like a thief in the night. The prepared man is the one who is faithful to his responsibilities.

1. The certainty of fulfillment. We have already looked at statements similar to the one found in verse 34 (see comments on 16:28). It is probably best to understand it as a reference to the terrible events which lie immediately ahead. The affirmation in verse 35 applies both to the prediction about the destruction of Jerusalem and to statements about the coming of the Son of man. The disciples can be sure that Jesus' words will be fulfilled.

2. The unknown time of the end. Believers may be certain that history is not eternal, that God is the sovereign Lord of history, and that the rule of God will one day vanquish completely the evil forces of the world. They may also have confidence that their security rests in God and that they will be saved to share in his eternal reign.

However, they cannot know when God is going to act decisively to bring history to a close. Faith in a God who is the Lord of history is a correct Christian attitude. Attempts to predict the future actions of God are futile and foolish enterprises for believers.

Jesus declared that "no one knows." He emphasized the impossibility of knowing the time of the end by adding "not even the angels of heaven, nor the Son, but the Father only." That is, they expected life to continue as they had always known it. They were forming new families, anticipating that they would rear their children in much the same way that they had been reared.

Now, there was nothing wrong with the activities mentioned by Jesus. Furthermore, the problem with the people in Noah's time was not that they were unaware of the time of the flood. Their problem was that they had left God out of their lives and were not living faithfully for him. According to the story, they were not destroyed because they did not know the time of the flood. They were destroyed because of their perverse commitment to evil.

So it will be at the end of the age. Men will be in the fields cultivating the crops. Women will be grinding the grain in order to prepare their daily bread. They will be judged in terms of their faithfulness to God and not because they are involved in ordinary activities when the end comes.

3. The coming as judgment. Jesus taught that the coming of the Son of man will be a judgment. And it will be a judgment which cuts across the lines of social relationships. Of the two men working in the field, one will be taken and the other left. Of the two women grinding grain, one will be taken and the other left.

The criteria for judgment, therefore, will be personal. It will have nothing to do with the categories of human society. It will ignore class, race, and social groups. The decision will be based upon the personal preparedness of each individual.

4. The necessity for preparedness. How is one to be ready for an event when he does not know when it is going to occur? The answer to that is simple. He must be ready at all times, beginning with the present moment.

Whatever God is going to do at any moment in the future,

he can do now. Every moment, therefore, has within it the possibility of being the last moment.

This is true also because of the very nature of human existence. History may go on for a year or ten thousand more. Individual human life, however, lasts at best for only seventy years or so. Many of us have already lived the greater part of our expected existence. Furthermore, none of us has any assurance that he will live another moment.

Life is a gift from God. It is given to us one moment at a time. Because our future is secure in God, we can accept every moment joyously and gratefully and live it responsibly.

If we want to do anything, we must do it now. This includes the all-important matter of trusting God and living for him. The way to be ready for the future is to be right with God now.

Jesus emphasized the need to be ready at every moment in his story of the thief. This may be an incident which had just happened in the village. While a family was sound asleep, a thief had broken into their house and made away with their possessions. We may be sure that the man of the house would have been prepared to resist him if he had only known when the thief was going to appear.

The Son of man will appear unexpectedly, like that thief who had surprised the householder. We cannot know when he is coming, but we do not have to be caught by surprise. We can be sure that we will be prepared when he comes if we are ready at every moment for his coming.

5. *How to be prepared.* How can one be prepared? That is a problem which many Christians seek to solve in the wrong way. They think that they can be prepared only by absorption with the coming of the Lord. So they spend their time studying the "signs of the times" to try to determine if he is about to come. Invariably they predict that we are living in the last days.

The believer is truly prepared for the future, however, when he is living responsibly for God in the present. The person who is living responsibly in the present does not have to be anxious about the time of the end, whether it is the coming of the Lord or his own personal end in death.

Jesus illustrated this truth by telling the parable of the good and bad servants. The good servant is the one who is faithful at all times to the wishes of his master. He discharges all his duties responsibly every day.

When his master returns, he receives his approbation. Since he has been faithful in his master's absence, he is given a position of greater trust and responsibility.

The bad servant, however, is the one who tries to guess when his master is going to return. The problem is that he cannot know the hour of his appearance and he guesses wrong. Instead of being a faithful steward, he abuses the trust placed in him by his master.

The consequences are inevitable. The master returns unexpectedly and sees for himself how his servant has abused the trust placed in him. The servant is punished swiftly and surely. His place is not with the faithful servants but with the "hypocrites." Indeed, he is the quintessential hypocrite—fawning and pretending when his master is present, but the exact opposite in his absence.

The real test, therefore, is not what people would do if they knew the Lord was returning. It is rather what they do in his absence. The grace of God is great so that even the "death bed confession" of the thief on the cross is accepted. So a person may be converted because he fears that the end is about to come. But a more genuine faith is that exercised by the person who lives each day faithfully knowing that he may live out his life in the world as it is.

The passage closes with Matthew's characteristic: "There men will weep and gnash their teeth." Weeping and gnashing of teeth are expressions of the tremendous frustration and sorrow of people who fully expect to be included by the Lord but who find themselves excluded at the decisive moment.

20.
I Do Not Know You

25:1-46

I. The Necessity of Being Prepared (Matt. 25:1-13)

Matthew 25 consists of three parables which teach the proper stance of the disciple in the view of the fact that he does not know the time of the end. This first parable is about ten maidens who are part of a wedding party. Five of them foolishly fail to bring enough oil for their lamps and are caught unprepared when the bridegroom comes.

1. The parable. One of the most joyous celebrations in a Palestinian town was a wedding party. Then, as now, it was very important and exciting to be a member of the party. This was especially true for the unmarried young ladies who were friends of the bride and who served as her bridesmaids. Ten such young ladies are depicted in Jesus' parable.

A procession was part of the wedding ceremony. The two bridal parties left their separate places of assembly and met at an agreed upon location. Then the two parties moved to the house of the bridegroom.

The young ladies in question were waiting for the procession accompanying the bridegroom. Since the procession was at night, the people who participated in it carried lamps to light the way. Evidently all of them would have had enough oil for their lamps if the bridegroom had arrived at the appointed hour. Five of them had not reckoned with the possibility of delay, however. This is why they are called foolish. Foolish indeed is the person who expects a wedding party of this kind to be on time.

Five of them had brought jugs with extra oil for their lamps in case of an unexpected delay. The other five maidens found that their lamps had used all their oil, and they had none with which to replenish them. Rebuffed when they requested oil from their companions, these maidens were forced to go in search of an additional supply. It was unlikely that stores would be open at such a late hour in the normal course of business. If the wedding was a large one, however, as it appears to have been, the whole village was probably awake to view the festivities. They could expect to find a shopkeeper who would consent to sell them oil.

By the time the maidens returned, the wedding party had reached its destination, and the door to the house was shut. When they asked to be admitted, they were refused. Their foolish lack of foresight caused them to miss the wedding.

2. Lessons from the parable. There are various points of interest in Jesus' story. One of these is the delay of the bridegroom. This detail suggests one of Matthew's major concerns. He was writing to point out the danger of making predictions about the returning of the Lord.

People who make predictions about the coming of the Lord put themselves in a potentially very difficult and dangerous situation. What will they do if their predictions do not come true, as is most likely? People have been indulging in these kinds of predictions since the church began. Up to this moment they have all been wrong.

Some of them have been able to rationalize their error, make adjustments, and continue to be believers. There is, however, the ever possible danger that people who are disappointed will lose faith.

It behooves Christians, therefore, to be ready for all eventualities. Since we do not know when the end will come for us, either by death or in some other way, the only wise position is to plan to live all our life for God. Then we shall not be surprised by any future eventuality.

Another lesson is seen in the point that the oil was not transferable. The wise maidens refused to share their oil, since they might not have enough for themselves. This is especially true when applied to the realm of spiritual preparation. No one can depend upon anybody else. We cannot borrow from the faith and dedication of others.

Faith in God and the faithfulness which flows from it are extremely personal and intimate matters. Neither devout father nor mother, neither believing wife nor friend has more than enough for himself. It cannot be borrowed from them in the hour of crisis.

Yet again, a person must be prepared before the unpredictable moment of crisis comes. When it does arrive, it is too late to make preparation for it.

All of us know of tragic illustrations which come from the lives of people who presumed that they had enough time to get ready for crisis. The young father, virile and strong, presumes that he has enough time to obtain insurance for his children before his death. But he is killed by an unexpected heart attack, and wife and children must suffer from his failure to be prepared.

The tragedy is heightened in matters affecting man's relationship with God. When should one trust him and begin to live for him? Tomorrow? How foolish it is to think that tomorrow belongs to us. Tomorrow is always potentially the day of crisis—the day when preparation can no longer be made. If there is anything that we must do, we must do it today. This is the only moment that God has given us. Since this is the only moment that God has given us, it should be the moment of decision and action.

II. Making Use of Talents (Matt. 25:14-30)

Through the parable of the talents Jesus teaches that disciples must be responsible in their use of capabilities. Two of the men who receive talents put them to work. One, however, buries his talent. When his lord returns from a trip, he condemns the servant and deprives him of the talent he has.

1. The parable. This story is about a man who is about to go on a trip and has to make arrangements to see that his business is carried on. He does so in a very unusual way. He distributes the responsibility for his wealth among three of his servants, to each according to his ability.

One servant received five talents, another two, and the third one. Since a talent weighed seventy-five pounds, the responsibility in each case was considerable. The exact value would depend upon the kind of metal involved, whether it was gold or silver.

Two of the servants used their talents in commerce and doubled their value. One, however, was afraid to risk anything. Therefore, he buried his for safe-keeping, a not uncommon procedure in a time when banking was very primitive. When the master returned, he called the servants in for an accounting. The two who had used the talents profitably received the approbation of their lord and were entrusted with even greater responsibility.

The third was in an embarassing position in comparison with the success of his fellows. He had gained nothing with his talent. In the manner of such persons he attempted to shift the blame for his lack of stewardship to his master. He had been afraid to risk losing his talent because he knew that his master was a hard, demanding man. His major concern, therefore, had been to keep the talent safe until his master returned.

Instead of receiving the approval that he evidently thought he deserved, the man was condemned by his master.

According to the master, there was a way open for even so cautious a man as this. He could have taken the low-risk venture of lending the talent for interest. He would not have doubled the talent. Since interest notes were high in the ancient world, however, he would have been able to show a nice profit. Because of the failure to make responsible use of his talent, the master took it from him. He had proved to be unworthy of trust.

2. *Lessons from the parable.*   We must keep in mind the central point of the parable. The way that we are to prepare for the future is to use faithfully and responsibly what we have in the present. Fear of the coming crisis of judgment is not to be the dominating concern of our lives. We must not be preoccupied with conservation. It is necessary to risk all without regard to the consequences and results. With this major truth in mind, it is certainly valid for us to see other truths in the parable.

Each person has a certain capacity for service. We are accustomed to calling these capacities talents because of this parable. Furthermore, the capacities or talents of God's servants differ. One has many talents, another has only one. It is important that we not judge ourselves with reference to others.

If we do compare our talents with those possessed by others, we are defeated from the start. There are really two primary dangers that arise from this kind of sinful comparison. One peril is that we shall be guilty of a baseless arrogance. We may feel that we are superior to our neighbor because, in our opinion, we have a greater capacity than he.

The second danger is that we shall feel inferior and inadequate because our talents are not as numerous as our neighbor's. The result is that we bury the talent that we have rather than use it.

We are not responsible for the number of talents we have. They come to us as God's gift. We are responsible for using what we do possess. God does not judge us in comparison to our fellow-man. He expects only that we use the gifts he has given to us in his service.

3. *The principle.*   The reward for the faithful use of talents is increased responsibility. This is an interesting point. One might think that the master would have allowed his servants to retire or at least that he would have given them a long vacation. But, no, he gives them more opportunity for service.

On the other hand, the man who fails to use his talent loses it. This is a law of life. The more one serves, the more capable he becomes for greater service. The less one uses his capacity, the more it will deteriorate and the less he will be able to do.

III. The Basis of Judgment (Matt. 25:31-46)

Jesus describes the role of the Son of man as judge. He will separate the sheep from the goats. The sheep, that is, the saved, are the people who have ministered to the hungry, thirsty, lonely, naked, sick, and imprisoned. The goats, that is the condemned, have failed to help needy people.

1. The judgment. Jesus picked up the title "Son of man" and applied it to himself. In the incarnation, however, he was a veiled Son of man, the exact opposite of the powerful, glorious figure involved in Daniel's view (Dan. 7:13). He had not appeared on the clouds accompanied by angels to overthrow the forces of evil. He had come into the world as one helpless, the victim of evil.

Jesus taught, however, that the future appearing of the Son of man would be different. He would come in power to exercise the functions of judgment. This judge is also called the King, that is, the King Messiah.

The judgment will be a time of separation. The figure used by Jesus must have evoked a well-known scene in the minds of his Palestinian listeners. They had seen shepherds separate their flocks. The sheep which were white were easily separated from black goats. Goats were highly prized in Semitic lands, and a man's wealth was reckoned by the number of goats in his flocks. There was no prejudice against them. Nevertheless, sheep became the symbol of the saved, perhaps because of their helplessness and absolute dependence on the shepherd.

The judgment is a time of discrimination. The sheep are separated and placed on the right hand, the place of honor and trust. They are invited to "inherit the kingdom." To inherit the kingdom is tantamount to recognition as a child of God. The sheep are the "sons of the kingdom," the people who share in the benefits and glory of God's rule.

This kingdom is said to have been "prepared before the foundation of the world." The events of the end are the working out of God's eternal, sovereign purpose. God does not have to resort to makeshift, contingency plans. As the eternal Lord of the universe, he does not have to alter his ultimate goals.

2. The basis of judgment. There is more to be said about man's relationship and responsibility to God than is said in this passage. However, the teaching of Jesus given here must be taken very seriously, and they have not always been given due attention.

Traditionally, evangelical Christians have taught that one's status in the future will be determined by one's relationship to Jesus Christ: "Believe on the Lord Jesus Christ, and you shall be saved." But an all-important question arises. What does it mean to believe in Jesus? From some of our evangelism and teaching, we might conclude that it means giving orthodox answers to a theological examination.

Sometimes we equate faithfulness to Jesus with attendance on religious service and giving money to support the institution, both of which are very important aspects of responsible Christian living. We honor Jesus who never said anything at all about building buildings by erecting ever larger and more magnificent structures.

If we do take his words seriously we shall surely testify to it by a shift of our emphasis from statistics and buildings to people in their need. We may be getting some answers ready for the final examination, but they are often answers to the wrong question. The Lord is not going to ask, "How many buildings did you build?" According to this passage, he is going to ask: "How many hungry people did you feed? How many sick people did you visit?"

3. Service to the King. How do people best express their gratitude to and love for their Lord? Is it by leaving air-conditioned homes and riding in air-conditioned cars to sit in air-conditioned buildings to sing: "Jesus paid it all"? There is no question but that genuine Christians will want to worship their God. There is also a need for the family of God to express their relationship by coming together in a spirit of love. Worship of the Lord who loves the unhappy and unfortunate is the highest kind of hypocrisy unless it is expressed in service for the very people whom he loves.

If you want to minister to Jesus, you have to minister to the sick, lonely, and oppressed people of the world in his name. The person who has no compassion for the world's needy is on the opposite side from his Lord. Between them is a great chasm.

4. *The surprise of the judgment.* In both cases the people are surprised at the King's decision. Those who are invited to share his rule were unaware that they had ever ministered to him. One of the characteristics of truly good people is their unawareness of their goodness. The tragic plight of another human being awakens their compassion. They help him with no ulterior motive in mind.

The people who are rejected by the king are equally surprised. "When did we see you hungry?" they ask. They would have been only too glad to receive the King with due honor and deference.

We would also hastily affirm that we would be only too glad to receive Jesus. If he were to make an appearance in our town, we would spare no effort to show him how much we honor and love him. Nobody would close his home to him or deny him anything if the opportunity were given to us to serve him.

But the truth is that he will not appear to us in his own person, to claim his due of love and service. He is in our midst in the person of the ill and alienated of society. Once in a while he even appears at our church house doors. We do not recognize him, because he is shabbily dressed or perhaps his skin is the wrong color. All too often we turn him away.

How many of us will perceive the meaning of those opportunities that we failed to grasp only when we hear: "As you did it not to one of the least of these, you did it not to me"?

How do we get ready for the coming of the Lord? By taking advantage of the opportunities which arise day by day to love and help people in his name.

21.
This Is My Body
26:1-75

I. The End Draws Near (Matt. 26:1-16)

Jesus predicts that he will die during the Passover. The Jewish leaders, however, decide to postpone his death because of their fear of stirring up the people. A woman anoints Jesus in Bethany with a very expensive ointment, and he says that it is an anointing for his burial. Judas agrees to deliver Jesus to the leaders for thirty pieces of silver.

1. A prediction by Jesus of his death. We have noted that Jesus began telling his disciples about his fate after the confession at Caesarea Philippi. Now he makes his final prediction which contains a new element. It affirms that Jesus will die at the time of the Passover. According to the unanimous witness of the Gospels, Jesus was crucified on a Friday. This statement about his death, therefore, was made on Tuesday.

Jesus not only says that he will be killed but he specifies the manner of his death. He will be crucified. This means that he anticipates death at the hands of the Romans, since Jews did not use crucifixion as a form of execution.

2. The plot of the leaders. The chief priests and elders were two of the groups represented on the Sanhedrin, the Jewish high council. It is not clear if Matthew means that the whole council or just a part of it convened at the palace of the high priest. The high priest at this time was Caiaphas who held the office in A.D. 18-36.

The leaders reached several conclusions in their meeting at the

216

residence of the high priest. They decided to have Jesus arrested and executed. His popularity was such, however, that they wanted to do it as quietly as possible. Having reached this conclusion, they decided that they must postpone the deed until after the feast. The feast included the Passover proper which was followed immediately by the seven day feast of Unleavened Bread.

The leaders were afraid that any move against the popular Jesus at this time would provide a spark which would ignite a "tumult" (a rebellion or insurrection) among the people. Nationalistic spirit was especially high during the Passover.

Of course, it is clear to the reader of Matthew that these leaders made a decision that they could not carry out. Jesus himself had already affirmed that he would be crucified at the Passover. No matter what decision the leaders make, they cannot change the course of events. They are part of a larger pattern but do not recognize it.

3. The anointing. Jesus and the disciples lodged at Bethany, located about a mile and a half east of Jerusalem, during these days of his last ministry in the capital. According to the story, Jesus was in the house of a man named Simon who was called the leper. We may assume that Simon's leprosy had healed, or he would not have been in contact with society.

While Jesus was in the house, an unnamed woman came up to him and anointed him with a costly ointment from an expensive jar made of alabaster. What was the reason for her act? Perhaps she intended to anoint him as king.

The act inspired resentment on the part of the disciples. They complained that the "ointment might have been sold for a large sum, and given to the poor." The disciples may have expected Jesus to agree with them, but surprisingly he did not.

Jesus reminded them: "You always have the poor with you." This does not mean that poverty is inevitable and that we should accept the condition of the poor. In fact, the statement made by Jesus should be taken in the opposite way. If the disciples were really concerned for the poor, they would have abundant opportunity to show their mercy to them. It was not their resentment to the woman but their continuing ministry to the poor that would be the test of their true attitudes.

There are occasions when lavish expressions of love, which may seem foolish or wasteful by logical standards, are appropriate. The woman's act was justified in the circumstances. Jesus was facing the supreme crisis of his ministry. The poor would always be with them, but men had only a short while to show their affection for him.

We have suggested that the woman may have intended to anoint Jesus for kingship. Be that as it may, Jesus interpreted the act in the light of his knowledge of his own destiny. The same ointment that could be used to anoint a ruler could also be used to prepare a body for burial. This is what Jesus said the woman had done for him. He predicted that future generations, unlike his disciples, would praise her act.

4. The betrayer. Another figure now enters the drama. He is Judas, one of the twelve. Judas agreed to deliver Jesus to his enemies. For his work he received thirty pieces of silver. Matthew literally says that "they weighed him out" thirty pieces of silver, for to him the sordid deed is foreshadowed in Zechariah 11:12. Whatever Judas' motive for betraying Jesus, however, it was probably more than sheer greed.

There are two questions and a crucial theological problem involved in the account of Judas' role in Jesus' arrest. The first question is: What did he actually do? He helped the leaders achieve their purpose of arresting Jesus in a way that would not provoke the mob. Since he was a member of the inner circle, he could lead Jesus' enemies to him when he was isolated from the crowds. This is in fact what he did when he led the group which arrested Jesus to Gethsemane. Because they had the cooperation of Judas, the religious leaders did not have to postpone their plot to bring about the death of Jesus.

The second question is: Why did Judas do it? We can only offer conjectures as to the reason Judas decided to become a tool of Jesus' enemies. It may well be that Judas was the first person to perceive that Jesus was not going to fulfill the dreams and political expectations of his disciples. The name Iscariot, according to some scholars, may indicate that Judas was a zealot. If so, he belonged to that fierce, radical sect of Judaism that advocated taking up arms against Rome. He may have followed Jesus in the conviction that he was the messianic King who would lead his people in the God-ordained revolt against their oppressors. Jesus, however, was not going to do that. Indeed, he was going to die. Rage and frustration may have driven Judas to the act of betrayal. Or, as some suggest, Judas may have intended to force Jesus' hand by precipitating a crisis which would make him issue a call to arms.

The theological problem raised by the Gospel accounts about Judas is a serious one. Was Judas nothing but a helpless puppet in a game that was played out in fulfillment of God's purpose? If such was the case, how can Judas be blamed for what he did?

The Scriptures teach that the death of Jesus was no accident. They also teach that the initiative in the events of the salvation-history incarnation always lay with God. Men thought that they were in charge, but they were badly mistaken. God was really in charge.

On the other hand, the Scriptures teach in various places that God is not the author of evil. Evil is rebellion against God and not the fulfillment of God's purpose. How can we reconcile the two, that is, the conviction that God is in charge with the conviction that God is good?

I think that we must begin with the belief that God is good and that he does not want men to do bad things. I do not believe that God's essential will for Judas was that he betray Jesus. God wanted Judas to respond to the Lord in love and obedience.

But men are evil and perverse. They are not good as God wants them to be. They are idolatrous; they are filled with hatred and prejudice. However, God is not defeated by man's evil. He prefers that men love and serve him. Nevertheless, if they rebel against him, God is not defeated. God will use even their evil to accomplish his redemptive purpose of love. So he uses men both in their obedience and in their rebellion. In either case, he achieves what he sets out to do.

Judas was not a helpless pawn, nor were the Jewish leaders, nor was Pilate. Their posture of rejection and blindness was self-chosen. God did not make Judas into an evil man. God did use Judas, however, even though he was evil.

After Judas agreed to cooperate with the leaders, the stage was set. All that was lacking was the "opportunity," and it soon appeared.

II. The Last Supper (Matt. 26:17-30)

At the last supper Jesus discloses that one of his disciples will betray him. During the celebration of the Passover he teaches that the bread and wine represent his body and blood.

1. Preparation for the Passover. For pilgrims who did not live in the city, it was necessary to secure a room from one of the residents of the city in which to celebrate the Passover. A sheep had to be purchased as well as wine and spices for the meal. The sheep, of course, had to be slaughtered in the Temple, and the meal had to be prepared. Matthew says that the disciples made these preparations.

At about 3:00 P.M. the slaughtering of the Passover sacrifices began in the Temple on Nisan 14. The feast itself began some time after 6:00 P.M., that is, on Nisan 15. The meal was served on low tables around which the company reclined on cushions. Our traditional image of the last supper comes largely from Da Vinci's painting which is not true to the situation.

The minimum number which could form a group or company to celebrate the Passover was ten. There were thirteen in the group presided over by Jesus. It was customary for a person in the group to act as the head of the company, as Jesus did in this case.

2. The betrayer.   Jesus knew what none of the disciples except Judas comprehended. One of that intimate circle of twelve men with whom he had shared his life during the preceding months was a traitor.

How did Jesus come to know that Judas would betray him? The narrative does not tell us, although it may imply supernatural knowledge. It may be that Jesus had detected a change in the demeanor of Judas. Or, someone could have informed on the treacherous disciple.

Following the declaration by Jesus that one of the group would betray him, the disciples begin to ask: "Is it I?" A more accurate translation of the question would read: "It is not I, Lord, is it?" There is some doubt in the disciples' question, but there is also hope. No one can be sure how he will stand up under severe testing. One can only hope that he will be equal to the situation, but he cannot predict that he will be.

The perversity of the sin is heightened by the statement: "He who has dipped his hand in the dish with me, will betray me." In any society a deed of this nature is reprehensible. To accept a man's hospitality, eat at his table, share his friendship, and then go out to double-cross him is the ultimate in perfidy. This was especially true in Semitic society where eating together had a much greater significance than it does among us.

During the Passover, every participant dipped bitter herbs into a sauce. So all the disciples, therefore, had dipped with Jesus in the dish. The traitor knew who he was, but he too asked the question: "Is it I, Master." Jesus' response showed Judas that he not only knew that one of the disciples would betray him; he also knew the identity of that disciple. "You have said so" means "yes."

Why did Jesus let Judas know that he was aware of his scheme?

It was perhaps one last effort to turn Judas from his evil—an effort that was futile. Perhaps Jesus' words were a shock to Judas, but that did not deter him from carrying out his evil compact with the religious leaders. We should be aware of the fact that many of us also have something of the character of Judas. How many of us have left the table of the Lord to act and speak in ways that betray our relationship to him?

3. The words of institution. The Lord's Supper was instituted in the context of a Passover feast. During the Passover, the blessing was spoken over the unleavened bread at the beginning of the main part of the meal. When Jesus gave thanks, broke the unleavened bread and distributed it, he was simply following the normal pattern for the feast. What is new is his statement about the meaning of the bread. As the disciples were receiving and eating the bread, Jesus declared: "This is my body."

In Aramaic, the language spoken by Jesus, there was no verb. The words of Jesus were: "This, my body." In other words, "this bread represents my body."

At the close of the main meal, the head of the family said grace over the cup of wine and passed it around to the family or company. This was the third of the four cups that figured in the complete Passover feast. As the disciples received the cup, Jesus interpreted its meaning: "This is (represents) my blood of the covenant." Some manuscripts have "new covenant." It is, of course, a new covenant, whether the word is present or not.

These two elements of the Passover were later separated by Christians from the original feast and became what we know as the Lord's Supper. In the early days of the gospel, it was probably observed in connection with a common meal, called the *agape* or love-feast. Subsequently, however, Christians dropped the practice of the common meal and retained the celebration of the Supper, using only the two elements of bread and wine.

4. The meaning of the supper. The Lord's Supper was instituted as a part of the Passover and took some of its meaning from this feast that celebrated the liberation of the children of Israel from Egypt. The specific act of salvation emphasized in the Passover was the salvation of Israelite children. According to the story, all the children in homes where blood had been sprinkled on the lintel and doorposts were saved from death (Ex. 12:21-27).

In New Testament thought, Jesus is the believer's Passover lamb. Through his sacrifice they are liberated from their spiritual bondage and from the power of death.

The supper underlines the truth that God has entered into a new covenant with his people through the death of Jesus. The words of institution are reminiscent of the words of Moses to the Israelites: "Behold the blood of the covenant which the Lord has made with you" (Ex. 24:8). The old covenant was initiated by God when he chose Israel to be his people. But God's choice was not unconditional. The people whom he had chosen were to respond to his grace by living lives of obedient love. The covenant was sealed through the sacrifice and the sprinkling of blood on the altar.

The new covenant, however, is initiated not by the slaughter of oxen but by the death of Jesus. Here God has come to meet man and to offer man a new relationship to him. And here man must come to meet God. He must recognize that his standing before God is determined by his position with reference to Jesus.

The blood of Jesus is poured out for the forgiveness of the sins of many. Technically crucifixion was a bloodless execution. The language of institution is determined by the sacrifical system of the Old Testament rather than by the actual fact of the crucifixion. But forgiveness is not obtained nor is salvation secured by the magical properties of blood. It is made possible through the self-giving of Jesus, through his death and not as a result of a magic trick. If we trust that God has gone to this extent to save us and if we turn to him as this loving, self-giving, saving God, he accepts us. The important matter is not how we are saved, but the fact that we are saved. All of us who are believers recognize that our salvation and relationship to God are possible through the death of Jesus on the cross, even if we cannot explain it.

There is another aspect to the words of institution which we must consider. Jesus himself did not participate in the meal with the disciples. He declared: "I shall not drink again of this fruit of the vine until that day when I drink it new with you in my Father's kingdom." While the disciples feasted, Jesus fasted. Perhaps his fast was motivated by the seriousness of the hour. This was no time for him to be eating. Perhaps it was a pledge of the certainty of the future. He would eat with them again—in the kingdom.

At any rate, the words indicate that the Supper not only looks back. It also looks forward. It is an earthly experience of a future heavenly fellowship. When believers gather around the table of the Lord, they do so with the joy of knowing that their fellowship has a future. They shall celebrate that fellowship in reunion with their Lord in the kingdom.

Jesus and his disciples ended the Passover meal by singing the second part of the Hallel (hymn) in accordance with the Passover ritual. Then they left the house in Jerusalem to go to the Mount of Olives.

III. Gethsemane (Matt. 26:30-46)

Jesus predicts that the disciples will desert him in the hour of crisis. Peter protests that he will never deny him. Jesus takes Peter, James, and John into Gethsemane where he prays for release from the suffering which lies ahead. The disciples sleep even though Jesus urges them to watch and pray that they enter not into temptation.

1. *The disciples' response to the approaching crisis.* In Zechariah 13:7 we read: "Strike the shepherd, that the sheep may be scattered."

Jesus' words in verse 31 are related to this passage from Zechariah. He sees the prophecy fulfilled in the events that lie just ahead. Jesus, the Shepherd of the flock will be smitten. As a result, the sheep—the disciples—will be scattered. Jesus predicts that the disciples will disintegrate in the crisis of his arrest and death. The prediction is followed, however, by a promise. He will go before them into Galilee. The shepherd will return to gather the scattered flock together and produce a new fellowship.

2. *Peter's protest.* Jesus' prediction produced a heated and emphatic denial from Peter. What Jesus had said might be true of the other disciples, but it was not true of Peter! There is a great deal of arrogance in Peter's remarks. He believed that he was made of sterner stuff than the others. "I will never fall away," he assured the Lord.

How do we account for Peter's subsequent failure in the light of his arrogant self-assurance at this moment? Perhaps one factor more than all others will explain it. Peter completely misunderstood the nature of the crisis. He still nurtured the conviction that Jesus was going to lead his disciples in a messianic revolt against Rome. He was willing to make any sacrifice in such a glorious venture.

Peter's arrogance was probably justified in the light of his vision of the future. He would probably have been willing to die in a struggle for power and glory. However, to follow Jesus in the path of rejection, humiliation, and weakness was an altogether different matter. To submit to abuse and vilification without striking back was something Peter was totally unprepared to do.

Moreover, Peter did not know himself as Jesus did. He saw himself as an heroic figure, a leader of men, a patriot for his nation. He was not aware of his own possibilities for weakness and failure. That others might fail—he was willing to admit. That he might fail—never!

Peter is a favorite figure in Christian thought because we are so much like him. His sins are our sins: seeing the faults of others but not our own, interpreting the gospel in terms of our own prejudices and ambitions, and failing so often to follow the Lord is self-giving love.

Not only would Peter deny the Lord. The denial would take place that very night. Peter would not deny Jesus once but three times before the cock crowed. In Roman time the cock crow was the third watch of the night, from midnight to 3 A.M. Jesus' statement, however, probably should be taken to mean that Peter's thrice repeated denial would occur before morning broke.

3. *Jesus faces death.* The place of Jesus' agony was Gethsemane, possibly one of his favorite retreats. The name means "oil press" and was probably derived from the fact that a press was there to process the olives produced in the grove.

The struggle in Gethsemane is one of the mysteries in the life of Jesus. What was the cause of Jesus' agony? Why did he shrink from the ordeal that lay ahead? Of one thing we may be sure; Jesus was not acting. The struggle was a real one. Mark uses even stronger words to describe Jesus' anguish than Matthew does. He says that Jesus was "greatly distressed and troubled" (Mark 14:33). Moffatt translated Mark's phrase with the words "appalled and agitated."

"This cup" signifies Jesus' suffering and death. He was no masochist who sought death. He begged God to spare him the terrible ordeal that lay immediately ahead. While no man can measure the depths of the Lord's anguish nor understand it clearly, it may be explained in part by the fact that he faced rejection by his own people. He loved them; he had given himself to them; he had opened to them the door of the kingdom. He felt their rejection intensely. Also, he knew that their rejection would lead to God's judgment upon the people. No wonder he asked God to find some other way.

Even in the midst of so great agony, however, Jesus still addresses God as "Father." Even when he is forced to walk a lonely terrifying road, he affirms the basic relationship between God and himself.

The way of escape from the crisis was so starkly simple. All

Jesus needed to do was to leave Gethsemane for some safe retreat. He could have saved himself, but in so doing he would have saved no one else. Gethsemane is the place where the drive to save one's self comes into direct conflict with God's call to give one's self. In such situations we generally choose to save ourselves. It is so easy to rationalize flight. But he chose to lose himself to save us. His prayer ends, therefore, as should every prayer offered by one who is committed to God: "Thy will be done."

4. *Watch and pray.* Jesus chose three men to share the hour of his lonely struggle—Peter, James, and John. These three constituted a kind of inner circle within the twelve.

To these three men Jesus gave his instructions: "Watch." He knew that the betrayer would soon lead his enemies into the sacred retreat. He wanted the disciples to be alert and to tell him when they came.

He told them also to pray. Their prayer was to be one of the petitions in the Lord's Prayer: "Lead us not into temptation." Temptation here has the meaning of "testing" or "trial." The disciples were unprepared for the trial so rapidly approaching, so their only recourse was to plead with God not to lead them into a situation with which they could not cope.

The words of Jesus indicate that the disciples are not all bad. "The spirit is willing." This means that their intentions are good; they really want to be faithful. "But the flesh is weak." That is, they will be unable to act on their commitment.

This is a description of the tension which all Christians have found in their experience. Many of us truly want to be good followers of Jesus, but in the time of testing we yield to peer group pressure. Or, the desire for success or money is so strong that we fail to do what we really want to do. Paul expressed the idea in another way: "I do not understand my own actions. For I do not what I want, but I do the very thing I hate" (Rom. 7:15).

The disciples slept instead of praying and were unprepared

for the crisis when it came. Finally Jesus' own struggle in prayer ended, the victory won. The hour of his suffering was upon him. The betrayer was on his way to the garden.

IV. The Arrest and Hearing Before Caiaphas (Matt. 26: 47-75)

When Judas identifies Jesus with a kiss, the men sent by the Jewish leaders to arrest Jesus seize him. One of the disciples attempts to resist with a sword and is reprimanded by Jesus. Then Jesus is led to the residence of Caiaphas, the high priest. Peter follows in order to observe what is going to happen. Jesus is accused by two witnesses of threatening to destroy the Temple. When he declares that he will be seated at the right hand of God, he is charged with blasphemy. Several persons identify Peter as a companion of Jesus. After he denies that he was associated with Jesus three times, the cock crows. Leaving the residence, Peter weeps bitterly.

1. The arrest. The crowd sent by the Jewish council to arrest Jesus did not know him. Since it would be difficult to identify him in the dark, Judas had told them to arrest the man whom he kissed.

The method chosen by Judas to betray Jesus shows the depths of his perfidy. He hailed him as "master," "rabbi," meaning "my teacher." It was a title expressing great respect. The kiss was commonly used by Jews at the moment of greeting. It was a sign of deep affection. No wonder that the kiss of Judas has become idiomatic for an act of the basest treachery—that of pretending love and respect for a person when one is seeking to harm him.

Jesus addressed Judas as "friend." We may be sure that this word was not spoken in irony or hypocrisy. The love of Jesus still reached out to his disciple even during the moment when the chasm between them had become so terribly wide.

The crowd had arrived to arrest Jesus armed with swords and

clubs. Likely they thought that the man whom they were after was a rebel leader with a dangerous group of followers.

Jesus knew the real reason for this foray in the night. Such a show of force was clearly unnecessary, since he was not a fugitive. To the contrary, he had been in the Temple teaching day after day where he could easily have been apprehended. But this was not a deed to be undertaken in the light of day when they would have to answer to the people for it. Sending out the armed crowd with instructions to arrest a dangerous revolutionary was a cowardly subterfuge. The word "robber" in verse 55 was used of nationalist guerillas who often covered up their lawlessness with the mask of patriotism. Jesus was not that kind of person, and his open, honest actions had proved it.

At least one unidentified follower of Jesus had a sword and used it, cutting off the ear of a slave of the high priest. Jesus, however, rejected this act of violence. Perhaps the man thought that he was doing Jesus a favor, striking the first blow in a glorious campaign of liberation. But Jesus had consistently rejected the way of violence. However enticing it might have been, he knew that it was the way of ultimate defeat: "All who take the sword will perish by the sword." He saw all too clearly what would happen to the Jewish people if they resorted to the sword in their desire to gain their freedom from Rome.

According to statements in verses 54 and 56, the experiences of Jesus were a fulfillment of Scripture. The Scripture alluded to here must be such passages as Isaiah 53 and Psalms 22 and 69.

2. The hearing before Caiaphas. From the Mishnah (a part of the Jewish Talmud) we learn that a trial before the Sanhedrin had to take place in the daytime. The hearing before Caiaphas, therefore, must have been an informal interrogation. It was held to see if any evidence that Jesus had broken the law could be found.

For a time the attempt was futile. Many witnesses came forward.

Evidently no two of them were in agreement. In Jewish legal practice a man could not be condemned unless at least two witnesses gave corroborating testimony against him. Finally two did come forward. They accused Jesus of threatening to destroy the Temple. Jesus had predicted the destruction of the Temple, but the testimony gave a distorted view of his teaching.

This accusation was hardly sufficient for the purposes of Jesus' enemies. They could not bring about his execution on that basis.

The defendant had a right to answer his accusers, a right which Jesus declined to exercise.

The high priest pressed for an admission from Jesus that could serve as the basis of an accusation against him. "I adjure you" means "I call on you to answer under oath." A claim by Jesus to be the Christ (Messiah) could be used against him. In Roman political circles a man who claimed to be the Messiah would be regarded as a revolutionary. At this point Jesus did reply: "You have said so" must mean "yes." Jesus shunned the use of the term Messiah because of its political implications. Although he seemed to accept the designation in this case, he proceeded to interpret it. The Messiah was not a political leader. He was the Son of man who would be seated "at the right hand of Power" (omnipotence). This was a Jewish circumlocution used to avoid mentioning the sacred name for God. The leaders did not have to fear an armed revolt from Jesus. Rather, they had to reckon on facing Jesus as Son of man who would come to them as the heavenly Judge.

The claim to a position at the right hand of God was interpreted as a claim to deity and, therefore, as blasphemy. Technically, this was not a correct interpretation of Jesus' statement because the name of God was not used. Blasphemy was punishable by death under Jewish law. It is doubtful, however, that the Jews had the right to administer capital punishment under the rule of the Roman procurator.

3. The denial by Peter. It is hard to understand the reason for Peter's following Jesus into the high priest's residence. In a sense he showed himself to be the most loyal of Jesus' followers, since the others had fled. Whatever our opinion of Peter's conduct during this critical hour, we must remember that he at least had the courage to follow Jesus, although "at a distance."

All the Gospels record a threefold accusation against Peter and his threefold denial. The denials increased in intensity. First, there was the simple declaration: "I do not know what you mean." The second time he made his declaration upon an oath. The third time he went further and invoked a curse on himself. This passage is a good example of the kind of thing Jesus had in mind when he forbade oaths (Matt. 5:34). An honest man does not need to support his statements upon an oath.

Peter's regional dialect betrayed the fact that he was a Galilean. It was only natural to infer that a Galilean was a follower of Jesus.

After the third denial the "cock crowed." The cock's crow may have been the sounding of the bugle in the Roman garrison at the end of the watch, about 3:00 A.M. The cock's crow brought Peter up short. The scene which had occurred only a few hours earlier flashed into his mind: a scene played out between an arrogant, brash disciple declaring his loyalty and a sad Jesus who knew that Peter could not stand up to this test. Overcome by remorse, "he went out and wept bitterly." This is the moment when grace can begin its work—when a man is stripped of his arrogance and stands before God naked in his need.

22.
They Crucified Him

27:1-66

I. The Trial Before Pilate (Matt. 27:1-26)

The council delivers Jesus to Pilate. Judas commits suicide, and the Jewish leaders use the money which they paid him to buy a field in which to bury foreigners. Pilate interrogates Jesus. Convinced of Jesus' innocence, the governor attempts to secure his release. He offers the people a choice between the release of Jesus and a notorious prisoner named Barabbas. They choose Barabbas. Pilate's wife, troubled by a dream, warns her husband not to condemn Jesus. Pressured by the crowd, Pilate decides to allow Jesus to be crucified. He washes his hands as a symbolic gesture of his innocence in the decision. The people accept responsibility for Jesus' death.

1. The role of the Sanhedrin. According to the notice in 27:1, "All the chief priests and elders of the people" met in a morning session to make plans for the death of Jesus. This evidently means that a full, legal meeting of the highest council took place in contrast to the informal hearing that had occurred during the night. Matthew does not say what plans were made. From what follows, however, we may conclude that they decided to seek to have Jesus condemned to death by Pilate, the Roman governor of Judea.

The Sanhedrin determined to accuse Jesus of being a dangerous rebel. As we have seen, the word Messiah had revolutionary implications. Roman officials had learned from experience that anyone who claimed to be the Jewish Messiah, or King, intended to attempt a revolution against Roman authority. Since it is doubtful that the council had the authority under Roman rule to hand down a capital sentence, this may have been the only way for the Jews to accomplish the goal of having Jesus executed.

2. The tragedy of Judas. We have suggested that Judas may have cooperated with the authorities to bring about the arrest of Jesus in order to force him to act. If this is true, Judas expected that Jesus would initiate his messianic campaign rather than be put to death. The statement in verse 3 fits this conjectured picture. Instead of resisting the authorities and leading the people in a revolt, however, Jesus was their helpless victim, destroyed on a Roman cross. "When Judas saw that he was condemned" implies that Judas had not anticipated this outcome.

Judas had committed a terrible sin. He had been involved in bringing about the condemnation and death of an innocent person. The narrative says that Judas repented, but this is not to be understood as the repentance which is essential to forgiveness. He simply wished that he had not committed the evil act and was filled with remorse for it. Nevertheless, he did not turn from his sin to God to ask forgiveness.

The money Judas had received for his treachery was a concrete reminder of his deed. He decided to return it to the men who had used him. Even there, however, he received no understanding or help. He had served the purpose of Jesus' enemies, but they were not at all concerned about what happened to the wretched man. Had they been true to their trust as teachers of the people, they could have pointed the way out of his despair, but they summarily dismissed him. He left, but not before he had thrown the price of betrayal at their feet "in the Temple." The story does not say where this took place in the Temple.

A burden of guilt produces despair. If it cannot be resolved, it becomes more than a man can stand and, thus, leads him to suicide. So Judas went out and hanged himself. The tragedy of

Judas is that it could have been different. Peter had also committed a terrible sin, but he discovered the secret of the gospel. There is no sin that God in his grace will not forgive.

The unexpected act of Judas presented the priests with a problem. They could not put "blood money" in the treasury, for it was unclean. What a vivid picture of the sin of the religious legalist! He is careful about observing all the rules but extremely insensitive to the real moral and ethical demands of God.

Judas dealt with his problem by hanging himself. The priests solved their problem by buying the potter's field as a burial ground for strangers. That is, it would be a place to bury people, perhaps foreigners, who died in Jerusalem and did not have a burial place of their own.

Matthew sees all this as a fulfillment of prophecy. He says that the prophecy is from Jeremiah but verse 9 is really a free paraphrase of Zechariah 11:13.

3. *Pilate the judge.*   The permanent residence of the Roman governors of Judea was in Caesarea, but they occasionally went to Jerusalem when the need arose. Pilate happened to be there at this time, and so he was available to hear the accusation against Jesus. The accused had the right to speak in his own defense, and Pilate gave Jesus that right. He asked him if he actually claimed to be the king of the Jews. Jesus answered: "You have said so." The terminology had been chosen by Pilate. Jesus himself did not use it, but he would not deny that he was in fact the Messiah. The answer was, therefore, a qualified "yes."

Jesus had answered Pilate, but he would not respond to his accusers. Probably they were setting forth the specific evidence upon which they based their charge. Why did Jesus not answer? Perhaps he knew that it was useless. Early Christians understood his conduct to be a fulfillment of the prophecy of Isaiah about God's Suffering Servant (see Isa. 53:7). Pilate was amazed, for he was not accustomed to seeing accused men who refused to answer their accusers.

The story makes it clear that Pilate was convinced of Jesus' innocence and wished to free him. This wish was reinforced by a warning from his wife. She had experienced troubling dreams and interpreted them as a warning from God. She transmitted the warning to her husband: "Have nothing to do with that righteous (innocent) man."

Pilate was in a dilemma. He needed the support of the Jewish high council in order to have a successful administration. At the same time, his duty under Roman law was to free the accused who were innocent.

He attempted to find a way out by using the custom of freeing a Jewish prisoner during the time of the Passover. This was a time of high nationalistic spirit when the crowd would be pleased by the release of a political prisoner.

Instead of releasing Jesus outright, however, he decided to give the people a choice. The decision then would be theirs. He offered to release either Barabbas or Jesus. We may suppose that he misjudged the situation and assumed that they would ask for Jesus. But the Jewish leaders had been working with the people to turn them against Jesus. Pilate's plan failed, therefore, when the people demanded the release of Barabbas and the crucifixion of Jesus.

Finally, in a pathetic gesture, Pilate washed his hands to symbolize his innocence in the death of Jesus. The crowd, eager by this time for Jesus' death, was glad to accept responsibility: "His blood be on us and on our children." Little did they realize the fateful consequences of their decision. No people have ever suffered as much as the Jewish people as a result of a tragic, wrong decision. The irony is that the decision with such far-reaching consequences was made by such a few.

Pilate released Barabbas and ordered Jesus to be scourged as a prelude to crucifixion. Criminals condemned to death could be beaten with a whip of knotted cords or leather strips which were sometimes weighted with pieces of metal to increase the agony. Men often died under this kind of torture.

4. Barabbas, the freed man. The man whom the people chose for release is an enigmatic figure. We may assume that he was one of the revolutionary guerillas who were such a vexing problem to the Roman authorities. It is even possible that he made some claims to messiahship. Ironically, he was probably guilty of the kind of crime for which Jesus died.

His name is suggestive. It means "son of a father." The true Barabbas, the genuine Son of the heavenly Father, was rejected for a false Barabbas. According to some manuscripts Barabbas' first name was Jesus (Joshua). This would make the irony of the people's choice even more vivid. Joshua means "the Lord saves." The people rejected the genuine Joshua for a false one.

II. The Crucifixion (Matt. 27:27-50)

The soldiers abuse and mock Jesus and then lead him away to be crucified. Simon of Cyrene is forced to carry Jesus' cross. After he is crucified at Golgotha, Jesus is mocked by passers-by and also by the religious leaders. The robbers with whom he was crucified also revile him. Jesus cries with a loud voice: "My God, my God, why hast thou forsaken me?" Then he dies.

1. The method of crucifixion. Execution by crucifixion was used by the Romans to punish slaves, criminals of the lowest sort, and rebels. Jesus was condemned to die in this way because he was accused of being a rebel. Crucifixion was an extremely cruel form of punishment. At the site of execution the upright stake was set in the ground prior to carrying out the sentence. The condemned man did not carry the entire cross, which would have been much too heavy. He carried the crossbeam.

Evidently Jesus was not able to carry the crossbeam, probably because he had been weakened by the scourging which he had endured. Simon, a man from Cyrene, was in Jerusalem, perhaps to participate in the Passover. He was pressed into service by the Roman soldiers and forced to carry the cross for Jesus. Mark identifies Simon as the father of Alexander and Rufus (Mark 15:21). They must have been Christians known to the community for whom Mark wrote. This leads to the conjecture that Simon himself may have become a convert as a result of his association with Jesus.

When a man was crucified, his arms were attached to the crossbeam with either thongs or nails. His body rested on a block attached to the upright post. His feet were either nailed or attached with thongs to the post.

Crucifixion was essentially a bloodless form of execution. The references to the blood of Jesus in the New Testament are due more to the analogy of his sacrifice with Old Testament sacrifices than to the actual fact of the crucifixion itself.

Death came to the crucified person with agonizing slowness, either from shock, exhaustion, or exposure. It sometimes took days for a condemned person to die. For this reason a squad of soldiers was detailed to guard him so that he could not be rescued before death. The condemned man was crucified naked, and the soldiers received his clothing as a bonus for their duty. Early Christians thought of the soldiers' getting Jesus' clothes as a fulfillment of Psalm 22:18.

Jesus was on the cross only a few hours before death came, which was itself manual. Perhaps he died so swiftly because of shock, produced not only by his execution but also by the previous beating that he had endured.

Jesus was executed at Golgotha which means "skull." We are not sure why it was given this name. It may have been simply because it was a hill shaped like a skull. Our word "Calvary" is a transliteration of *Calvaria*, the Latin equivalent of Golgotha found in the Vulgate, a Latin translation of the Bible.

2. The mocking of Jesus. Christian readers of the gospel are aware of the irony in the response of various groups to Jesus. Those who mocked him were saying more than they knew. Before the soldiers led Jesus away to be crucified, they had their moment of cruel sport. They clothed his bleeding body in the scarlet robe of royalty, pressed a crown of thorns on his head, and put a reed as a mock scepter in his hand. What a pitiful figure he must have made before them, this pretended "King of the Jews." How could this helpless man be a king? If they had only known that he was not only King of the Jews but Lord of the universe!

The passersby added their insults after Jesus had been crucified. He had promised so much—he had said he would destroy the Temple and build it up in three days. But he could do so little—he did not even have the power to come down from the cross. Little did they know that his power would be demonstrated in an even more sovereign way. He would not come down from the cross, but he would emerge from the tomb victorious over death.

The Jewish leaders were present to enjoy their victory over Jesus. They derided him: "He saved others, himself he cannot save." Truer words were never spoken, nor was a more genuine prophetic insight ever uttered! He who would save others cannot save himself. The way of redeeming love is the way of self-giving sacrifice. The contrast between Jesus and sinful men becomes unmistakeably vivid at this moment. The leaders had saved themselves by protecting their institutions from the threat of Jesus' prophetic words of judgment. In seeking to save their lives, however, they had lost them.

3. *Jesus on the cross.*   After he was crucified, Jesus was offered wine. It was a Jewish custom to offer a condemned man either pure wine or wine mixed with an opiate to deaden his pain. Matthew alone tells us that the wine was "mingled with gall" for he sees this act as a fulfillment of Psalm 69:21.

Jesus refused the wine. He would drink this cup of suffering with a clear head, accepting nothing to relieve the pain.

Another remarkable aspect of Jesus' bearing was his silence under the taunts of the people around him. He had taught that men should not repay evil for evil, and he lived out his own teaching in the most difficult of circumstances. While they taunted him, he was dying for them—an example that we who claim to be his followers would do well to remember.

Matthew tells us that while Jesus was on the cross, there was darkness over the land from the sixth to the ninth hour, that is, from 12:00 noon until 3:00 P.M. The darkness was symbolic of the judgment of God on the nation for its rejection of the Messiah.

The only word from Jesus on the cross reported by Matthew is often called the cry of dereliction: "My God, my God, why hast thou forsaken me?" This cry, which is a quotation of Psalm 22:1, is one of the mysteries of the crucifixion. What did Jesus mean? We can only guess. The meaning of the incarnation is that Jesus fully identified with us in our humanity. He was tempted at every point as we are (Heb. 4:15). It is a common human experience to suffer from a sense of alienation and terrible weakness when the tide of suffering overwhelms us. If he was tempted at this moment as we are, he was tempted to lose nerve, to have a sense of being utterly defeated.

Yet, as the writer affirms, he was without sin. Even at this moment he did not lose faith in God. At the moment of desolation he still said, "My God."

Another suggestion arises from the content of Psalm 22. While Jesus quoted only the first verse of Psalm 22, he possibly had the whole psalm in mind. It begins with a complaint but it ends with an affirmation of faith. Jewish people had long gained comfort from this psalm in time of great suffering. So Jesus may have quoted from it to express his invincible faith in God in spite of the horrors of the moment.

The onlookers misunderstood the cry. Perhaps in his agony Jesus had not pronounced his words clearly. The people understood that he was calling on Elijah, who was thought to be the rescuer of the righteous in their hour of distress. Someone, perhaps a merciful gesture, offered Jesus vinegar to drink to relieve his thirst. Vinegar probably refers to a sour wine drunk by Roman soldiers. But others prevented the act. "Let us see," they said, "whether

Elijah will come to save him." No one was coming to save him, however, and in a short while he died. Matthew says that he "yielded up his spirit," probably to underline the voluntary nature of his death.

III. The Burial of Jesus (Matt. 27:51-66)

The death of Jesus is accompanied by supernatural phenomena—splitting of the veil in the Temple, an earthquake, and the resurrection of some dead persons. Joseph of Arimethea asks Pilate for the body of Jesus and buries it in his own tomb. Pilate grants the request made by priests and Pharisees that the tomb be secured against possible theft of the body of Jesus' disciples.

1. The supernatural portents. Matthew tells about two symbolic occurences which followed the death of Jesus. The curtain of the Temple was torn in two. In the Temple there were two curtains, one hanging at the entrance to the sanctuary and the other at the entrance to the Holy of Holies. It was the latter that was torn. The splitting of the veil in the Temple symbolized the truth that Jesus through his death had opened the way to God.

Also, an earthquake caused some tombs to open, and some of the saints—the people of God—were raised from the dead. This symbolized the truth that the people who belong to Jesus share in his triumph over death. His resurrection is the guarantee of theirs.

The portents surrounding the death of Jesus filled the Roman guards with awe. They called Jesus "Son of God." By this the pagan soldiers meant that Jesus was a divine hero or a demigod.

2. The witness. Matthew mentions several women who followed Jesus from Galilee (vv. 55-56), watched him die from a distance, and saw him buried (v. 61). Witnesses were very important to guarantee the truth of the gospel in succeeding years. It was very important that there were people who could affirm from personal experience that the Jesus whom they had followed in Galilee had really died, that he had really been buried, and that this same Jesus was the one who was raised from the dead.

3. The burial of Jesus. The law taught that an executed man's body should not "remain all night upon the tree" because it would "defile the land" (Deut. 21:23). Joseph of Arimethea, therefore, requested of Pilate that he be allowed to take the body of Jesus and bury it before nightfall. He then placed the body in a clean linen shroud (a normal burial custom), and laid it in his own new tomb. The dead were generally buried in natural or artificial caves outside the city. The tomb in which Jesus was buried was new, meaning that it had just recently been hewn out of the rock. The stone placed in front of the tomb was probably circular in shape so that it could be rolled back and forth.

4. The watch on the tomb. The day of Jesus' burial is called "the day of Preparation" (v. 62). This was Friday, the day when preparation was made for the sabbath. Matthew tells us that the chief priests and Pharisees, fearful of a hoax, went to Pilate on the sabbath to request that the tomb be made secure. They wanted to make sure that the disciples did not steal him and then claim that he had risen from the dead in accordance with his own prediction. Pilate granted their request.

The enemies of Jesus had done everything they could. They had brought about the death of Jesus. They even had the stone which closed the tomb sealed and guards before it. On that sabbath they celebrated their triumph while the scattered disciples wept over their shattered dreams.

23.
He Is Risen
28:1-20

I. The Resurrection (Matt. 28:1-15)

Two women followers of Jesus visit his tomb early on the first day of the week. The stone has been rolled away from the tomb, and an angel seated upon it announces to them that Jesus has risen. As they go to tell the disciples, they are met by the risen Lord. In the meantime, the guards report to the Jewish leaders that the tomb is empty. The leaders bribe them to report that the disciples had stolen his body.

1. The empty tomb. Jesus had been crucified on Friday and placed in Joseph's tomb just before dark when the sabbath began. Mary Magdalene and the other Mary had watched the burial, but they could not return to visit the tomb the next day because it was against the Jewish oral tradition to travel more than a sabbath day's journey, somewhat more than half a mile. According to Matthew the same two women came back to the tomb "toward dawn," as soon as it was light enough to see the way. The other Gospels tell of additional visitors to the tomb from among the disciples.

The two women found that the stone had been rolled away from the opening and that an angel was seated upon it. The expected reaction to such a supernatural event was fear. The guards were overcome with terror. The women were also afraid, but the angel responded to their fear with a word of reassurance.

The empty tomb, therefore, had a double-edged significance.

There was no word to relieve the terror of the guards, nor could there have been. The fact that Jesus had risen should be greeted with fear by his enemies. They thought they had done away with him. He would no longer be around to trouble them. The way that you get rid of a man is by killing him. Or so they thought. How mistaken they were. They were not free of him. Their sense of victory was an illusion. He had rendered their momentary triumph void by emerging from the tomb. The worst that they could do to him was not enough. Now they had to deal with a living Jesus, the powerful conqueror of death.

For the disciples, however, the knowledge that Jesus was alive was an antidote to fear. They could begin to reinterpret their precarious position in the world in the light of his unexpected triumph. Their situation in the world was completely altered, for their Lord's victory over death became the guarantee of their own future. They could emerge from their hiding places where they had cowered in fear and despair throughout the long sabbath of his interment. They belonged to one who had shown them that the path through death leads to life for God's people.

2. *The meaning of the empty tomb.*   The fact that the tomb was empty was not enough to prove that Jesus was alive. The enemies of Jesus knew this and conspired with the guards to spread a falsehood. They were to report that the disciples had stolen the body of Jesus. This kind of story was still being used to combat the message of the gospel in Matthew's own time. Other explanations to account for the absence of the body of Jesus from the tomb continue to be given to the present.

An empty tomb is not proof of a resurrection. This is clear. But the fact that it was empty is important to the gospel. If there had been a body in that tomb, it would have been an effective barrier to belief in the resurrection.

One of the most convincing proofs that Jesus was no longer dead is that his body was not produced by his enemies. Just a few days after his death his disciples began to preach that he was alive. One perfect answer to that preaching would have been to counter the disciples' claims with the undeniable evidence of a corpse.

Some people teach that the story of the empty tomb is a legend produced by the Christian community. They say that Paul, for example, nowhere mentions an empty tomb. This is true. Paul announced that Jesus died and was buried. Then he affirmed that Jesus was raised from the dead (1 Cor. 15:3-4). Now, he could hardly have claimed that the Lord had risen if he believed that he had remained buried. He does not say specifically that the tomb was empty, but his words can hardly mean anything else.

3. The risen Lord. The story of the empty tomb is told in the Gospels, but it is not used elsewhere in the New Testament as proof of the resurrection. Paul cites various appearances of Jesus to believers as the evidence that he had really been raised from the dead (1 Cor. 15:5 ff). By appearing to the women, Jesus showed them that what they had hardly dared to believe was actually true. He was alive. They now had something to report other than that they had not found his body in the tomb and that an angel had assured them of his resurrection. They had seen Jesus himself.

The resurrection of Jesus altered the relationship between him and his disciples. He had become their exalted Lord. The women fell to the ground to worship him. We do not know when worship on the Lord's day became a general and accepted custom. We know that the Christians in Corinth met on the first day of the week (1 Cor. 16:2), but the information in the New Testament on the subject is scanty. Matthew, however, describes here the very first Christian worship service on the first of the week. We continue to meet on Sunday to celebrate his resurrection.

4. The message to the disciples. The resurrection of Jesus is not to be kept a secret. It must be shared. The angel had instructed the women to tell the disciples that Jesus had risen from the dead. They had been running to do that when they met Jesus.

He repeated the angel's instructions.

The words of Jesus are interesting. He calls the disciples his "brothers." The use of that word speaks forcefully of his love and grace. In his last experience with them, the disciples had forsaken and denied him. Now he reaches out across their sin and guilt to reclaim them with the word "brother." He sees not only what they are but also what they will be. "Brother" speaks of his incredible love, steadfast in the face of injury and rejection. It is also prophetic. That patient love will begin its work in their lives and help them to start all over again.

Luke and John record appearances in Jerusalem. For Matthew, however, the significant appearance took place in Galilee. Jesus told the women to instruct the disciples to go to Galilee. Jesus' words which repeat the angel's message (v. 7) remind us of his assurance to his disciples on the night of his arrest (Matt. 26:32).

Jesus would not go with the disciples to Galilee.

He would go before them. Their journey, therefore, was an act of faith. They had to go without him, believing that they would see him when they arrived. One cannot help but wonder if they were tempted to doubt the message and not make the trip.

II. The Appearance to the Eleven (Matt. 28:16-20)

In accordance with Jesus' instructions to them, the disciples go to the mountain in Galilee where they meet him. There he commissions them to engage in a worldwide mission of evangelism and teaching.

1. The disciples' reaction to Jesus. The mountain where Jesus appeared to the eleven disciples is not identified in Matthew. One may speculate that it was the mountain where he gave the great sermon or the mountain where he was transfigured, but there is no evidence to support the speculation.

There was a twofold reaction to the appearance of Jesus. The disciples worshiped him, as the women had done when they met him. By this Matthew meant full Christian worship which expressed a new attitude toward Jesus as the risen One.

Some of the disciples, however, doubted. We are not to suppose that all the disciples were completely convinced of the truth of the resurrection at the same time and to the same extent. Not even an appearance of Jesus could remove all doubt. Some of them must have wondered if there were not some other explanation for this unusual experience.

2. The authority of Jesus. The Gospel of Matthew began with a claim for Jesus. He was the son of David, the true messianic King. It closes with an even higher assertion of his kingship. Jesus is the sovereign Lord of the universe, possessed of unlimited authority over it.

The "therefore" of the Great Commission is based upon his regal authority. More than any other king he has a right to expect his disciples to obey him. The world belongs to him; he has the authority to send his representatives to every part of it. Christian missionaries have always known that national and cultural boundaries are to be ignored in carrying out the wishes of their king. No earthly authority has the right to exclude messengers of this King from his territory.

Finally, of course, the promise of Jesus is secured by his authority. Men can have faith in his promise because he has the power to fulfill it. He is a King who not only sends his subjects on missions but accompanies them.

3. The mission of the church. Interpreters have often pointed out that there is only one imperative in Jesus' commission. It is the command: "Make disciples." The first part of the commission is a participle "going." It can be translated "As you go, make disciples."

It is true that people are very much on the go, especially in our modern, mobile world. They do not have to be commanded to go. But the important matter for Christians is what they do in their going. There are usually more lay church members than missionaries in any country of the world. Sadly, however, these Christians are generally not doing what the Lord commanded. They are not witnessing to the gospel as they go.

Students of Greek also know that a participle can be imperatival in force. The versions of the New Testament are not necessarily wrong, therefore, when they translate the participle as an imperative: "Go." The mission field for the Christian is the world. The decision for Christian vocation must be made in the context of a world, all of which needs the gospel. Many Christians who are sensitive to their responsibility will be led by God to spend their lives in lands and cultures other than their own in carrying out the Great Commission.

The central part of Jesus' commission to his church is found in the command: "Make disciples." A Christian disciple is a person who acknowledges Jesus as his Lord and who follows him no matter what the cost. As we have seen, there are no boundaries to the mission of the church. Therefore, there can be no classes or divisions based upon race or culture within the church. Jesus had in view a world community of believers in which the pagan structures of race, class, wealth, and culture no longer play a part. The only important factor in a genuine Christian's attitude toward another man is his relationship to Christ. Is he not a believer? Then it is my responsibility to witness to him about the Lord whose love reaches out also to him. Is he a believer? Then he is my brother in Christ, a subject of the heavenly King, a member of a new race being formed from every kindred and tribe.

Those who respond to the claims of the King, therefore, are to be "baptized in the name of the Father and of the Son and of the Holy Spirit." The formula elsewhere in the New Testament is "in the name of Jesus." There is no essential difference. Name stands for the person. To be baptized in the name of Jesus means to be baptized as one who belongs to him. A relationship with Jesus, however, is understood in the New Testament as a rela-

tionship to God. The trinitarian formula simply makes this conviction more explicit. Believers are to be baptized into the possession
of God as he is known to the Christian, that is, as Father, Son,
and Spirit. The believer baptized in the name of Jesus belongs
no less to God than he who is baptized in the name of the triune
God. After all, what is important is not the words said over the
baptized person. It is the fact that he belongs to God because
of his own personal decision for him.

The converts are to be taught, but we must be careful not
to equate being a disciple with the intellectual mastery of material.
What they are to be taught, for example, is the Sermon on the
Mount. What is important is not whether we memorize the Sermon
but whether we live by it. So Christianity is not a new gnosticism,
as some would make it. We are not saved by knowledge, nor
is our Christian life to be measured by it. We often hear someone
remark of another person: "He really knows the Bible." But that
is not the crucial matter. Does he live by it? Is he a follower
of Jesus Christ in love, forgiveness, and courage?

4. *The promise.*   The Christian disciple does not walk alone.
He is not left only with a memory of a person and his teachings.
He is also conscious of a presence. The Lord who gave the Sermon
on the Mount and who commands men to engage in a world
mission of the church is also known as the Lord who is present
with his people.

In the midst of persecution and sorrow, in the hour of rejection
and loneliness there is One who walks with them.

This promise is without limitation. Jesus will be with his flock
"to the close of the age." So long as this present age lasts with
its evil and its tensions, with its sorrows and its losses, he will
be a comforting, strengthening, illuminating presence in their lives.